HONEST SEO

DEMYSTIFYING THE GOOGLE ALGORITHM TO HELP YOU

🔍 **GET MORE TRAFFIC & REVENUE**

JASON HENNESSEY

AN INC.
ORIGINAL

An Inc. Original
New York, New York
www.anincoriginal.com

This work is being published under the An Inc. Original imprint by an exclusive arrangement with *Inc. Magazine*. *Inc. Magazine* and the Inc. logo are registered trademarks of Mansueto Ventures, LLC. The An Inc. Original logo is a wholly owned trademark of Mansueto Ventures, LLC.

Distributed by Greenleaf Book Group.

For ordering information or special discounts for bulk purchases, please contact Greenleaf Book Group at PO Box 91869, Austin, TX 78709, 512.891.6100.

Design and composition by Greenleaf Book Group
Cover design by Greenleaf Book Group

Publisher's Cataloging-in-Publication data is available.

Print ISBN: 978-1-63909-016-7

eBook ISBN: 978-1-63909-017-4

To offset the number of trees consumed in the printing of our books, Greenleaf donates a portion of the proceeds from each printing to the Arbor Day Foundation. Greenleaf Book Group has replaced over 50,000 trees since 2007.

Printed in the United States of America on acid-free paper

23 24 25 26 27 28 29 30   10 9 8 7 6 5 4 3 2 1

First Edition

For my wife, Bridget,
and children, JJ, Zach, and Brooklynn,
who still have no idea what I do for a living
but continuously support all
my crazy ideas.

Contents

SEO unleashes

BUSINESS VALUE!

Introduction

No matter what kind of business you have, Search Engine Optimization (SEO) and digital marketing are vital efforts you must continuously make to remain competitive in the digital age.

SEO

Search Engine Optimization (SEO) is a set of ongoing practices designed to improve the appearance and position of web pages in organic search results. It is the process of continuously improving your site's organic rankings on search engines such as Google, YouTube, Amazon, and Bing. In practice, SEO typically involves creating high-quality content, monitoring your site's technical health, building links from other sites, making sure your site loads quickly, and providing a good user experience by making your site easy to use and navigate.

You might be surprised to hear that before I became a digital marketing expert, I was a radio personality. I was also a DJ. And I served in the United States Air Force. But the most surprising part of my journey is that, 20 years ago, I started a wedding directory service for brides in Las Vegas.

Starting that directory might've been the single most important decision in my life (next to meeting my wife and deciding to have kids), because it started my journey into digital marketing.

At first, I had someone develop a website. This was when Google was a newborn. I didn't have many people visiting my website, so I told the website developer that something was broken. He introduced me to the term "Search Engine Optimization." I'd never heard of it before.

I taught myself how to do SEO before any of the cool kids knew what SEO was. I bought a thick book about SEO and learned the basics, one chapter at a time. Twenty years later, I'm still working in the SEO field. I've fallen in love with every facet of the business.

It's funny how some things change your life. And I'm hoping this book will change your life, too. With the skills, ideas, and knowledge contained in this book, you'll be able to take any site, any business, or any venture, and scale it, grow it, and attract traffic.

One of my clients, a lawyer, told me over the phone, "The jury returned a $25 million verdict in a case that came from a website lead." That client trusted the SEO strategy I developed for them and netted millions of dollars from a single lead, as well as got justice for the family involved.

Whether your business involves representing $25 million legal cases or selling $7 ebooks doesn't matter. Website traffic can change everything about your business. Right now, there's an ocean of potential clients, buyers, consumers, and leads who want your services or products. They're out there, but they can't find you. And when they search for someone like you, chances are a competitor is showing up in the Google search above you. Chances are, you're not even on their radar.

The truth is that the best products don't always win. It's the best marketers who get the attention your business needs.

The good news is you can be the best *and* get more business—you can have both. SEO will increase the visibility of your website to attract more customers. Unlike the broad, unfocused reach of a billboard or other traditional advertising methods, SEO empowers you to target exactly the type of leads you want, down to the specific keywords they're searching for on Google.

Furthermore, if you use my proven SEO strategy (the same strategy we use at my agency, Hennessey Digital), then you can generate traffic worth thousands or millions of dollars in equivalent Google-paid ads. You have the strategies from a $10,000-per-month agency all in one book.

Done right, SEO will pay for itself.

FORGET WHAT YOU THINK YOU KNOW ABOUT SEO

It may be difficult to get a clear definition of SEO because it can appear complicated, expensive, and overwhelming at times. If that's you, you might just want to know where to start.

Perhaps you've read some blog posts on SEO and only found

yourself more confused. While there's a lot of good, clear content, there's also a lot of bad information out there. With so many self-proclaimed SEO experts and gurus on the internet, it's easy to be led down the wrong path.

This book gives you a blueprint to help you put the theories of SEO strategy into action. I've included practical steps you can take right now and put into practice for the future as well. In this book, I'll teach you how to:

- Understand SEO fundamentals
- Design and engineer your website's blueprint and architecture
- Recruit a digital marketing team and hold them accountable
- Measure the success of your SEO efforts
- Drum up press for your business that creates stronger SEO
- Create a targeted content strategy
- Apply advanced SEO techniques to your website

I'm going to break down SEO using simple explanations that work whether you're a one-person business or a fast-growing startup. If you're intimidated by SEO, don't be—it's simpler than it seems.

CONTENT STRATEGY

Content strategy is the ongoing process of developing a comprehensive plan to ideate, design, create, share, and promote content that aligns with your brand, speaks to your target audience, and is measured against specific goals.

Before working with my agency, many of my clients visited a bookstore, asked the clerk for a book about SEO, and were pointed toward the computer engineering section. They tentatively cracked open a book, only to be overwhelmed with technical jargon and more details than any entrepreneur needs to know.

This isn't that kind of book. SEO doesn't have to be complicated, and you don't need to be a coder to understand and master it. In fact, I don't even code myself.

WORKING IN SEO SINCE THE BEGINNING

SEO became a discipline in the late 1990s, and by 2001, I had immersed myself in the field. Since then, I've spent most of my adult life reverse engineering Google's algorithm—figuring out exactly why Google ranks web pages the way it does. What does Google measure? What does it value? Why is one web page ranked higher than another? What can you do to make your website reach more eyes? I found the answers.

SEO is a rapidly developing field, so I want to make the point that this book is meant to be evergreen, focusing on the principles that last.

There are so many blogs to read and keep up with. It's a chore to keep track of all the tactics from one well-intentioned blog to the next. And I know that sometimes it can be hard to know whom to trust—something I wish were different.

This book is designed to be the single holistic, end-to-end resource you can rely on. It's the foundation that'll set up all your efforts to come.

I've built a name and reputation as one of the go-to digital marketing experts for law firms, one of the most competitive and expensive niches in the world. I've also done it with online casinos and poker sites, where the difference between a #1 and #2 ranking on Google was $250,000 in daily revenue. If you learn how to implement my proven SEO strategy, you'll dominate your market—and you'll get more leads.

So if you're ready to start, there's only one thing left to do: keep reading.

the

SEO

Basics

CHAPTER 1

What Is SEO?

Opening this book, you might have a rough idea of what SEO means. You know it's a series of actions you can take to make your business more popular and more profitable. Maybe you've read countless blogs, and none of their advice had any impact. Maybe you've read a book about SEO, but you didn't really know how to act on the advice. And maybe you've even paid experts to handle your SEO, but nothing really changed. One thing is certain: you do not want to waste your time or your money.

I can tell you what SEO *doesn't* stand for: it's not the "same excuses over and over." My kids would groan at the dad joke (don't worry, I have more), but it's true. SEO has gotten a bad rap over the years. If you've taken advice from ineffective experts on the internet, or you're simply left clueless as to how all of this works, I understand. But done right, SEO is a worthwhile investment that can deliver an exponential return on the value you put into it.

SEO is relatively young. It's only been around since the late 1990s, so your competitors might not be leveraging it yet. Therefore, becoming savvy in this new frontier can give you a significant competitive advantage over other businesses that aren't investing in optimizing their websites. Even though it's hard to remember what life was like before we had Google, the internet is still young and evolving, and gaining an advantage in SEO can set up your business for years to come.

If there's a time to take action, it's now. You need to meet your leads where they are: on the internet. And how do they find you on the internet? By ranking on the first page of a search when someone types in those keywords.

THE SEO BASICS

SEO stands for "Search Engine Optimization." It's the practice of optimizing your website to increase your traffic and get in front of targeted prospects at the precise time they are looking for it. Your business offers a solution, and your website connects prospects and their needs to your solution. Whether you're a wedding photographer, affiliate marketer, or plastic surgeon, SEO is just a means to strengthen the connection between you and the people who need what you offer right now.

There are many search engines that people use to find content on the internet, but in this book, I'll be focusing on the one with the largest audience: Google.

Google dominates approximately 87 percent of the search engine market and web traffic. If a potential client searches for your consultancy, about nine out of ten times they're using Google. Google's algorithm factors in hundreds of variables to rate and rank web pages, which it returns to users as search results in a matter of seconds. You can control some of these variables; others, you cannot.

Think of applying SEO principles to your website like maintaining your lawn. What can you do to make it greener? You can water it. You can apply fertilizer. You can mow the grass once a week. These are all inputs you control to get your desired output—green grass. One thing you can't control is the sun, but you can adjust your behavior accordingly.

With SEO, just like maintaining your lawn, you will focus on the inputs you *can* control to achieve your desired output of more traffic and more leads. The three primary inputs you can control are site integrity, relevancy, and popularity, which I cover in detail in chapter 3. The uncontrollable element—the sun—is Google itself. Fortunately, while you can't control Google's algorithm, you can predict how it will act.

All of Google's decisions reliably work toward two ends: increasing profits while providing a good user experience for its clients. Google wants people to continue using its search engine, which means it wants to promote content that answers users' questions and helps solve their problems.

Seen from the user's perspective, the easier it is to find useful information on Google, the more you'll use it. And, considering that Google has an 87 percent market share, it has done a pretty good job of this. As seen from *your* perspective, the more user-friendly and helpful you make your website, the higher it will rank in the search results.

WHITE HAT VERSUS BLACK HAT SEO

Google's underlying algorithm produces its search results, and that algorithm changes constantly. Due to this constant change, it's critical to develop an SEO strategy that builds a lasting foundation of real value. You want your website to provide relevant information and solutions to problems for Google to consistently rank your content and direct targeted traffic to your website.

To build a solid foundation, you must engage in what is known as "white hat" SEO strategies, not "black hat" strategies. White hat SEO refers to strategies that adhere to the terms and conditions set by Google and other search engines. Black hat SEO, on the other hand, uses shortcuts and tricks to game the system, often by exploiting the algorithm to secure higher search rankings in a shorter period of time. However, in doing so, you risk getting your website penalized by Google. Yes, there really is a Google jail.

Generally speaking, black hat SEO can get you quick results, but whatever boosts your website gains may be short-lived. It would be a real shame to invest a lot of money in SEO only to see your website get penalized the next time Google updates its algorithm. By penalized, I mean removed from Google's listings completely.

White hat SEO is sustainable, scalable, and perennial. White hat strategies might take longer to implement and build upon, but the foundation you create for your website will be lasting and effective. It's worthwhile to do SEO right.

A final word about black hat SEO: if it hasn't happened already, at some point, you might read an article or watch a video that promises you a fast path to the top of Google's search results. There's a lot of great advice out there—but there's also a lot of black hat SEO practitioners, and it makes sense to be wary. Just like with dieting and investments, if it sounds too good to be true, then it is. Use your discretion (and the principles in this book), and you'll be able to tell the difference.

A PROVEN STRATEGY

How can you make your website as user-friendly—and Google-friendly—as possible?

The proven strategy I teach starts with reverse engineering the websites that are currently ranking in the top three search positions in your market. You want to see what's working for your competitors and, later, apply those strengths to your website. Do this preliminary planning work before you even start thinking about the design for your website.

SEO is a continual investment, not something you should start and stop. This isn't a one-and-done strategy—it's your website's forever strategy. Think of SEO like a retirement fund. The value continues to compound month over month. On the other hand, pay-per-click ads are more like day trading. You may get quick wins but could also just be investing in marketing campaigns with little to no return. While they are different, both are great digital marketing strategies if executed correctly.

SEO MEANS MORE THAN HIRING A WEB DEVELOPER

A common misconception among people new to SEO is to think, "I'll hire a web developer and pay them $5,000, and that will be that." But SEO is an ongoing process. It requires more work than a single web developer doing a one-time audit of your website. It's more than simply getting a domain on GoDaddy and checking the box that promises that your site will include SEO (an upsell you don't need).

In my experience, most web developers and designers don't have SEO knowledge. You might get emails from SEO "gurus" claiming that they can boost your website's search ranking for a flat fee, but be cautious. I get those emails, too. One-shot efforts may help, but my goal with this book is to educate and empower you so that you won't get taken advantage of.

I often hear from my clients in the law profession who tell me how their former SEO company would send them reports boasting a lower bounce rate or higher conversion rate, yet they would leave the meeting perplexed. They didn't see an increase in the number of leads and signed cases, which is the real barometer of success. That's because an agency can spin any metric to sound like good news if you don't understand the technical terminology. And whether you're hiring a consultant or an entire agency to help you improve your SEO, what matters in the end is whether you achieve your goals.

SHOULD I DO THIS ON MY OWN OR WITH A TEAM?

You might be wondering whether you should do this on your own or hire a team. Regardless of the scale, the right answer depends on who you are, what your goals are, and where you're currently at. If you're a college student with no money to spare, then hiring an agency probably doesn't make sense. But if you're a 25-person startup with a decent marketing budget, then maybe it does.

The best way to understand the problem is to break it down into three variables: budget, interest, and time. If you're cash-strapped but you have a lot of time plus a lot of interest, then maybe you can do much of the heavy lifting yourself.

However, there's a cap to how much you can grow on your own. SEO requires a multifaceted skill set—writing, publicity, design, coding, and more. I strongly encourage most businesses to hire a person or a team that can help them advance their SEO efforts.

I especially encourage hiring someone if you don't have an interest in the subject, you don't have a lot of time, and you do have a budget. At Hennessey Digital, the biggest key to our success is that I was able to hire the right people in the right roles. I cannot overstate the difference this makes to a business and its importance to the business's overall trajectory.

Don't worry about making a decision quite yet. In the chapters to come, I break down the basics of SEO further. Wherever you are in your entrepreneurial journey, I've got your back.

And if you know you want to hire someone, feel free to skip to chapter 5, where I break down the process of building a team in detail.

HOW MUCH DOES SEO COST?

If a $5,000 one-time fee isn't going to cut it, how much *does* SEO cost?

It costs as much as it needs to. It depends on your market, your competition, and the search terms (often known as keywords) you are competing for. If your business operates in a market with a lot of competition, it will cost much more than it would in a smaller market.

When you search Google for businesses in your market today, who shows up? The businesses that currently rank highest in your market are your competition, and they've had a head start. Most likely they've invested in their SEO for several years already, and you will likely need to spend as much or more to take their market share. Alternatively, you might be able to use more advanced strategies to move the needle faster. There are also some domains and search terms that have so much popularity and authority that they're nearly impossible to outrank. For example, there isn't enough money in the world to try to compete with Wikipedia at this point. They've laid far too much groundwork and have millions of pages of content indexed on Google. Fortunately, you don't need to compete with Wikipedia—you only need to compete with other businesses in your specific market.

Your business likely has several competitors that are taking SEO seriously, and they're fighting for the top three positions on the search results page. That's the goal: to rank in the top three positions for your target keywords, or at the very least make it to the first page.

As a popular SEO joke goes: "Where do you hid dead bodies? On the second page of Google."

My kids might cringe at that joke too, but statistics show that click-through rates drop dramatically the further down the search results you go. When a web page gets pushed to the second page, the traffic drops to almost zero. Most users will rephrase their search query and get a fresh list of results instead of going to the second page, so it's critical to secure one of those top three spots.

Your competitors play a significant role in how much you'll need to spend on SEO. They're the ones you need to outrank. However, if you operate in a smaller or less competitive market, SEO might cost less than you expect.

For example, maybe your business specializes in orthopedic shoes for children, and you find that the market in your area is wide open. Nobody has dominated that space online. In this scenario, a few thousand dollars per month might be enough to develop a strategy to secure the top search result for "orthopedic shoes for children" and start converting more sales and earning more revenue. Meanwhile, that same investment wouldn't be enough to impact a business trying to compete for the keyword "running shoes," where you have large businesses spending millions of dollars per month on their marketing. Whatever you need to spend per month to compete in your market might seem high, but when done right, SEO can deliver a significant return on your investment.

As a word of warning, if an SEO company offers you set pricing structures along the lines of "bronze, silver, or gold," I would be cautious. Generally, this pricing structure implies a one-size-fits-all level of service and pricing. Services and pricing expectations for SEO should be customized for your specific business depending on your market and competition.

CONTENT IS KEY TO YOUR STRATEGY

A large part of this strategy will revolve around writing, optimizing, and publishing content to your website. Google values fresh content and even rewards sites that publish articles on a regular basis. Creating a content strategy that identifies the publication frequency and keywords is important. I've seen sites lose their rankings and traffic by not being consistent with their content strategy. This is vital to maintaining your positioning in the search engine results pages (SERPs)—those pages that appear after someone enters a search term in Google.

SERP

The search engine results page (SERP) is the page displaying the results of a search for a particular keyword in a search engine.

Why the emphasis on content? I've always said, "Content is the food that Google eats."

Think about how Google makes its money: it serves ads on search results. If you're regularly publishing fresh content, you're providing more inventory for Google to serve additional ads and increase its profits. Google even has a "freshness algorithm" that promotes breaking news and current events, which will often jump to the top of the search results and temporarily rank above popular sites like Wikipedia.

By leveraging Google's algorithm and regularly publishing fresh content, you'll increase your search rankings and traffic while building an asset that will exponentially grow over time.

Q TIPS AND TAKEAWAYS: SEO

→ Search Engine Optimization (SEO) is the art of making slight adjustments to your website to increase your positioning in the search engine results pages (SERPs).

→ It can be difficult and frustrating to differentiate the self-proclaimed experts who take advantage of people versus experienced and ethical professionals who demonstrate consistently proven results.

→ SEO requires ongoing work to maintain and increase your Google ranking, so a single web developer or one-time solution may not cut it.

→ The cost of SEO depends on your market and competition. If your business operates in a competitive market, it will cost more to outrank the websites currently holding the top three positions.

→ Regularly publishing content is key to your SEO strategy and will help your website appear higher in search results.

Google

Q |

Google Search   I'm Feeling Lucky

CHAPTER 2

Behind the Scenes of the Google Algorithm

What happens when you type a keyword or phrase into Google? In a split second, the search engine returns a list of web pages relevant to the search query. But it's not magic returning the search results—it's a very complex proprietary algorithm.

The algorithm scans all the pages in Google's index and decides which ones to display to you. While the algorithm is complicated, the idea behind search rankings is simple: a higher search ranking equals more traffic, leads, and revenue for your company. In other words, if you understand how Google's algorithm works, you can leverage it to increase your rankings, get more leads, and grow revenue for your business.

THE ALGORITHM BREAKDOWN

Let's look at how Google's algorithm assigns value. Why does it rank one website higher than another?

When users have a good browsing experience, they stay on pages longer and view more ads. To that end, the algorithm values site elements that create a positive user experience, attract new viewers, and keep people browsing.

Google examines hundreds of variables and rewards websites that, among other things:

- Publish high-quality content on a regular basis
- Load quickly, preferably under three seconds
- Deliver relevant information that satisfies the searcher's intent
- Offer a safe and secure browsing experience
- Use a responsive design that is user-friendly on both mobile and desktop

In order to rank pages in the search engine results pages (SERPs), the algorithm looks at each page within its index, which Google refers to as documents. Then it asks questions such as the following:

- Do keywords from the search terms appear in the page's body copy, URL, or title tags?
- Is the page from a high-quality, trusted source?
- How old is the domain? When will it expire?
- How many links go to and from the page?
- How quickly did the page load?
- How much time do visitors spend on the web page?

The algorithm considers the search terms and returns the best pages that satisfy the criteria outlined in the questions. As you'll see throughout this book, every aspect of your website factors into Google's algorithm to determine where your site ranks. Google monitors the user's experience and makes adjustments to the search results every day. So in order to rank highly, your website must meet the requirements listed previously, deliver a great user experience, and continue to publish fresh content.

NEW CONTENT BOOSTS YOUR SEARCH RANKING

One of the best ways to get Google to "crawl" and index your website more frequently is by publishing new content. Every time you update your website by publishing new content, Google will visit it to see what has changed. Google maintains a carbon copy of almost the entire internet, and it's constantly "crawling" the web to keep its index up to date.

CRAWL AND INDEX

Crawl—Most of Google's search index is built through the work of software known as crawlers. These automatically visit publicly accessible web pages and follow links on those pages, much like you would if you were browsing content on the web. They go from page to page and store information about what they find on these pages and other publicly accessible content in Google's search index.

Index—A page is indexed by Google if it has been visited by the Google crawler ("Googlebot"), analyzed for content and meaning, and stored in the Google index.

This maintenance takes place behind the scenes, but what happens on the user's end?

When a Google search returns a list of pages, you're seeing a snapshot of the internet, not a real-time scan. Google has already used software programs called spiders to crawl the web, follow links, collect information on pages, and create an index. Google uses a very complex algorithm to organize and rank the data and then determines what will best satisfy the user's intent for that particular search.

Google wants its snapshot to be as accurate to the real-time web as possible, but it can't monitor the entire web simultaneously. It prioritizes where to send its spiders by looking at how frequently a website gets updated.

Publishing new content is a powerful trigger that draws Google's spiders back to crawl your website again and again. It's why Google crawls websites like **cnn.com** constantly—the unending stream of news reports feeds the algorithm's hunger for content. In turn, Google ranks the site highly.

Your website probably won't be as active as CNN's, but you should aim to post new content regularly. The algorithm wants to promote actively maintained websites, not sites that haven't been updated in years. If you add new pages frequently, it signals to Google that you take your website seriously, and you are rewarded with higher rankings and more traffic.

TECHNICAL ELEMENTS MAKE YOUR WEBSITE "CRAWLABLE"

Publishing fresh content keeps you on Google's radar. It's critical to your overall web strategy, but your website won't benefit from your efforts if Google can't index your pages. Your website must also be technically sound so Google's crawlers can scan it for information without any blockers.

What is Google looking at when it crawls your website?

A few of the most important technical elements that impact your Google search ranking include these:

- **Secure sockets layer (SSL) certificate**, which indicates whether your website is secure or not

- **Site speed**, which is how fast your website loads

- **Server-level performance**, which is whether your pages load without error

- **Domain age**, which is the length of time your website has existed

- **Domain expiration date**, which is how much time remains before your website's registration expires

- **Internal and external duplicate content problems**, which are what occur when a site plagiarizes content already indexed on Google

TECHNICAL WEBSITE PROBLEMS TO AVOID

Many websites fail to rank highly because they have poor technical SEO—any element that impedes Google's ability to navigate the website. Here are a few examples:

- Broken internal links
- Links to pages that no longer exist
- Large, uncompressed images that slow down the website

These problems detract from your website's ranking because they waste Google's resources. Google crawls the web by traveling from link to link, so the algorithm doesn't gain any useful information when it tries to follow a broken link. It hits a dead end. For example, if you've ever loaded a web page and seen "404 Error," it means the page no longer exists. Google penalizes this inefficiency by docking the offending website's search ranking.

So make sure your links are active by testing them regularly.

SEARCH RANK

It's easy to add a feature to your website assuming it will improve the user experience and boost your search ranking, but sometimes these additions actually do just the opposite.

For example, pop-ups are a common feature on many businesses' websites. The feature works by displaying a call-to-action window (whether to buy a product or sign up for an email list). We've all dealt with pop-ups, and they do get higher conversions (especially when you look at the data). So with that said, it's good to use them, right?

Not entirely. If the pop-up itself is very small, doesn't take up a lot of space (so it looks more like a banner), or shows up later in the user's browsing experience (not immediately after you click to the website), you might be fine.

The problem is that large pop-ups can be annoying, intrusive, and lead to a bad user experience—and Google knows this. Google calls features like this "intrusive interstitials" and may lower your search rankings if you use them.

Plugins or features that place these pop-ups on your website usually won't mention these issues, so it's up to you to think about whether a feature helps or hurts the user experience. Don't get me wrong: there are plenty of pop-ups that adhere to Google's guidelines and work really well. But some are better than others, so it helps to do your homework before putting one on your website.

THE ALGORITHM ASSIGNS A "PAGERANK"

Google's algorithm examines hundreds of inputs, including the ones described above, and uses the data to calculate different scores. One of the most important is called "PageRank." PageRank—named after Larry Page, Google's co-founder alongside Sergey Brin—measures the popularity and relative value of a web page, which factors into the web page's overall placement in a list of search results.

PageRank estimates a web page's importance by looking at the quality, relevancy, and number of inbound links pointing to it. For example, if you sell health supplements and a prestigious medical journal links to your company's website, it will have a much greater impact than a link from your friend who owns a locksmith company. One is more popular and relevant to your website's content, and the other is not.

In the past, Google made PageRank visible so website owners could see how their web pages scored, but they have since obscured these scores. Fortunately, tools like Moz and Ahrefs will approximate PageRank, so you can still get a good estimate of how your pages compare. Google's PageRank score ranges from 0-10, becoming exponentially higher (a logarithmic scale) as the score rises. Still, many of the third-party tools function on a 1-100 scale.

Before you start making any changes to your website, I recommend using a tool to approximate its PageRank. This will give you a baseline for tracking improvements to your website's popularity and performance as you start to map out your SEO strategy.

EVERY ASPECT OF YOUR WEBSITE MATTERS

The most important thing you need to know about Google's algorithm at this point is that everything about your website matters. The content, update frequency, technical aspects, design, user experience, links, and more all contribute to how Google ranks your web pages.

Remember, Google wants users to have a good experience and find the information they need, and it will reward websites that comply. By understanding how Google's algorithm works, you can be more proactive with your SEO strategy and reach as many potential clients as possible.

→ Google uses an algorithm that examines hundreds of variables to determine the best search results to return for any search term.

→ The search results you see aren't generated in real time but are a snapshot of Google's index.

→ Google creates this index by constantly crawling the internet using software programs called spiders.

→ Google's algorithm rewards websites that provide useful, relevant information and a user-friendly browsing experience.

→ Your website must be free of technical errors so Google can easily crawl it for new information.

→ Regularly publishing content will increase your rankings and traffic.

RELEVANCY

POPULARITY

INTEGRITY

CHAPTER 3

The Three Main Components of SEO

While Google looks at hundreds of variables and crawls your website, everything its algorithm considers can be boiled down to three questions:

- Is your content relevant to the particular search query?
- What is the popularity of your website?
- Is it secure, trustworthy, and accessible?

RELEVANCY

Google wants to provide users with answers to their questions or solutions to their problems as quickly as possible, which is why it measures the *relevancy* of web pages in relation to a search query. Relevancy simply measures the extent to which the content on a web page addresses the user's intent for a specific keyword or phrase.

To determine relevancy, Google looks at many variables, such as these:

- How many times a keyword appears on a web page, known as keyword density.
- How many other relevant websites link to that page.
- The keywords used in the anchor text of the link. Anchor text is the word or words attached to a link. Usually, anchor text appears underlined and in blue font.
- Behavioral patterns such as how long users spend on the page.

When someone clicks onto a page and stays there for six minutes, we can assume the content is interesting or useful to them. However, if they click on a page and then quickly leave after just a few seconds and go back to the Google search results to click on another page, which is commonly referred to as "pogo-sticking," the content probably didn't satisfy the user's intent for that particular search.

KEYWORD DENSITY, ANCHOR TEXT, AND POGO-STICKING

Keyword density, also called **keyword frequency**, is the number of times a specific keyword appears on a web page compared to the total word count.

Anchor text is the words that are displayed in a hyperlink when linking to another location on the web. It usually appears as blue underlined text.

Pogo-sticking is an SEO term used to describe a situation where a searcher quickly returns to the search page and navigates back and forth between pages in search results.

POPULARITY

To estimate the authority and importance of a website, Google takes *popularity* very seriously. As I describe in the previous chapter, they use something called PageRank to rank web pages in their search engine results.

The idea is that important websites are likely to receive more links from other websites. Not all links are equal, though. For example, a link from a respected university would have a higher PageRank than a link originating from an obscure mommy blog. To prevent gaming the system, Google frowns upon link trading ("I'll link to your website if you link to mine, and we'll both get a boost.") Google values one-way links more than reciprocal links.

You'll want to build links naturally by getting mentioned in the press or by contributing content as a thought leader on authoritative websites such as *Forbes, Entrepreneur,* and *Inc.* We cover this in greater detail in chapter 9.

INTEGRITY

Technical SEO, or a website's *integrity*, is the third component Google considers when ranking web pages within their index. This is an area of SEO that can be intimidating but is crucial to the success of your digital marketing strategy.

Bottom line: you will need someone who knows technical SEO and can assess if there are any technical blockers impeding Google from crawling and indexing your website. A website with high integrity will be secure, load quickly, and follow best-practice on-page technical SEO. It won't have broken links, internal or external duplicate content, unnecessary redirects, or issues preventing users from browsing on a tablet or a mobile device.

In short, a high-integrity website won't have any technical problems that detract from the user experience or make it difficult for Google to crawl its pages.

TOP-RANKING WEBSITES HAVE ALL THREE

Relevancy, popularity, and integrity each play a critical role in your website's SEO success, but more than any single factor, it's the *combination* of these three categories that will determine your website's search ranking.

To demonstrate how all three qualities are necessary to rank high on Google, let's imagine that you open your laptop and search for "blueberry pancake recipe." The first page quickly returns 10 excellent recipes, but you have your own recipe you want to share. You create a web page for your pancake recipe and wait to see what happens.

There's not much more you can do to make your recipe more relevant than any others, so you can check *relevancy* off your list. But even though your content is completely *relevant* to the search "blueberry pancake recipe," it's not *popular*. Nobody is visiting your website yet.

You manage to get on the cooking show *Top Chef* and receive a ton of exposure. News stories and blogs link back to your website. *CNN* publishes an article declaring that you have the greatest blueberry pancake recipe in the world.

Now your website is extremely *popular* and *relevant*, but there's a problem: your server isn't set up to handle such a high volume of visitors. Your website slows to a crawl and goes down entirely. It lacks the *integrity* necessary to rank high on Google.

Next, you fix your website's technical issues by addressing the server volume issues. Finally, your website has the SEO trifecta of relevancy, popularity, and integrity. Google recognizes these criteria, and before long, your recipe rises to the first page of search results for the term "blueberry pancake recipe," and you start receiving hundreds of thousands of visits to your website every month.

Often, websites will compete for the top three positions in Google's search results—perhaps one page is more relevant to a keyword, but another page is more popular. Google will then use behavioral patterns and signals of the user conducting the search to adjust the algorithm accordingly, and it will place the web page that consistently satisfies the user's intent higher in the search engine results pages (SERPs). In other words, the actions of the user contribute to Google's interpretation of the content of that page to place it in the search result positions. By ensuring you've achieved the trifecta of relevancy, popularity, and integrity, you're setting your site up to be at a top position in a Google search.

GOOGLE MUST CONSTANTLY OUTSMART MALICIOUS WEBSITES

Why doesn't Google simply rank the most popular or the most relevant websites the highest? Why take this more complicated three-pronged approach?

The answer is they used to, but over the years, their engineers have made necessary adjustments to their ranking strategy. It must constantly outsmart individuals who try to take advantage of the algorithm (see "black hat SEO" in chapter 1).

As an example, in 2010 an online eyeglass e-commerce website called DecorMyEyes was allegedly accused of treating customers horribly, failing to ship orders, and outright stealing money. The company received a large amount of bad press, but this negative attention started to benefit the website in terms of Google rankings and traffic. The company's owner knew that the more press the company received and the more links from trusted sources pointed back to his website, the higher the website would rank on Google and the more money he would make.

At the time, Google's algorithm put more emphasis on a website's popularity as a ranking signal without giving due consideration to other factors, like the company's reputation or the sentiment of the press. So when *The New York Times* wrote an article condemning the company, the algorithm misinterpreted it as a highly reputable media source vouching for the company by way of a link. The more negative attention and links the company earned from trusted sources, the higher they ranked on Google for competitive keywords, which increased their rankings, traffic, and sales.

Google then changed its algorithm to detract from companies with poor reputations, and the algorithm has only grown more sophisticated over the years, making it harder for people to manipulate it. The change in the algorithm is both a blessing and a curse. It's a blessing because malicious SEO practitioners now have a much harder time gaming the system. It's also a curse because it makes the algorithm more complicated, and the obfuscation on Google's part about how it works makes it more difficult to raise the visibility of your website. But that's why I wrote this book: to help you leverage and understand it.

HOW OFTEN DOES GOOGLE'S ALGORITHM CHANGE?

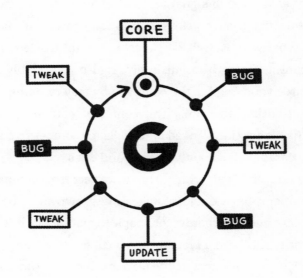

The story of the eyewear company is just one example of Google updating its algorithm to work more efficiently, produce better results, or combat manipulation. However, these kinds of changes happen all the time.

A month rarely passes without an update being made, and while many are simple bug fixes or minor algorithm tweaks, every once in a while, Google releases a significant update—commonly referred to as a "core update"—that shakes the SEO world. What kinds of changes does Google make?

One of the most notable core updates Google made to its algorithm was called Panda. Released in 2011, Panda aimed to reduce the amount of thin, low-quality content being published on the internet. Prior to the update, the algorithm relied too heavily on a site's authority without taking into consideration the relevancy and quality of the content. For example, highly authoritative and popular publishers like

Huffington Post would put up short web pages for common search terms, such as "When does the Super Bowl start?"

The web page would contain short, thin content, and the overall website wasn't relevant to football, and yet Google found these pages ranking higher than the NFL itself. Panda fixed the issue by rewarding high-quality content that kept visitors' attention for longer and pushed down thin, irrelevant pages.

However, it didn't take long until Google required another update to combat bad behavior. After Panda, the Penguin update came out in 2012 to address unnatural and artificial link-building techniques to manipulate search results. The Penguin update was aimed at decreasing search engine rankings of websites that violated Google's webmaster guidelines.

Before Penguin, people would successfully use many link-building strategies that used spammy backlinks. The strategy would be to find a forum or blog and leave a spammy comment with a link back to their own (usually unrelated) website.

For example, you might be on a forum about Ferraris when you suddenly see a comment advertising an online course for entrepreneurs with a link to their website. This strategy worked because in crawling the Ferrari forum, Google would follow the link and boost the popularity of the website featuring the online course, based upon the authority of the Ferrari website and the anchor text (words) used in that link, but not necessarily the relevancy of the link to the Ferrari website. Google fixed the problem with the Penguin update by penalizing websites that engaged in this type of activity.

You might ask, "With so many updates, won't I need to constantly adjust my website and SEO strategy?"

The answer is no, not fundamentally. SEO requires ongoing effort as you publish new content and build new links. However, the good news is that if you follow the strategy in this book and adhere to white hat SEO practices, your rankings and traffic will continue to grow and compound exponentially, regardless of whatever changes Google makes.

At the end of the day, Google's algorithm is designed to retrieve and order search results to provide the most relevant and dependable sources of data possible. Google just wants to provide the best possible user experience that will keep people coming back. As long as your website adheres to the guidelines referenced in this chapter, you should have nothing to worry about.

WHY THIS BOOK IS PERENNIAL

If you search for books on SEO, you'll find that many of them have to be updated for different years. You might've noticed that this book doesn't have a year attached to it. I've designed this book and the strategies inside to be perennial so you don't have to read a new book every year.

SEO is like building a house. Right now, you're building the foundation of the house. The material in this book forms the strategies and tactics that will last you a lifetime. Everything else—the finer details, SEO updates, etc.—is more like choosing which wallpaper you want in your living room. It can be important, but the most important thing is to focus on making sure the whole house is built securely.

You'll pick up more of these newer details on your journey. And if you're interested, I write about the cutting edge of SEO frequently at **JasonHennessey.com**, as well as in premiere publications like *Forbes*, *Entrepreneur*, *Inc.*, **iloveseo.com**, and *Search Engine Journal*.

TIPS AND TAKEAWAYS: RELEVANCY, POPULARITY, AND INTEGRITY

→ Relevancy measures the degree to which the content on a web page relates to a Google user's search term.

→ Popularity is determined by how many links point back to a web page and the authority of those originating websites.

→ Integrity refers to a website's technical components, including page-loading speed, crawlability, mobile responsiveness, and the lack or presence of broken links, among other things.

→ High-ranking websites will have all three components: relevancy, popularity, and integrity.

→ Google constantly updates its algorithm to counteract attempts to manipulate or cheat the ranking system.

→ Google wants your website to be fast, easy to use, and informative. As long as you practice an ongoing SEO strategy that creates a good user experience and follows Google's rules—like the one in this book—your website should be able to keep up with algorithm changes.

SEO

BLUEPRINT

CHAPTER 4

Creating the Blueprint for Your Overall Web Strategy

By now, you might be eager to dive into more fun and familiar territory, like the colors and logo of your website's design. But design comes way down the line, well after more important tasks. Website design is like home decorating, and we're still architecting the blueprint. Just like you would never build a house without laying a foundation, you don't want to build a website without first creating your strategy, either.

You've been operating without a plan until now, but it's time to change that. At this point in the process, you'll create your SEO road-map and preplan your content strategy and website architecture.

Before creating your strategy, I want to share the top four reasons SEO efforts fail to produce positive results. These are traps you can easily avoid if you know what to expect.

Failure reason #1: Treating it like a one-and-done

The first and most common reason for failure is treating SEO like a one-and-done project. People who make this mistake typically hire a web designer or developer who builds them a beautiful website and then checks SEO off their list. However, while most web designers and developers may have a basic understanding of SEO, generally speaking, SEO is probably not their true passion or core competency. They might apply some of the SEO 101 basics to your website and tell you it is good to go, but in reality, they are just 10 percent of the way there. SEO requires ongoing effort: regular content publishing, link building, and technical maintenance to stay competitive in your market.

Failure reason #2: Careless blogging

The second mistake people make is assuming they need a blog on their website and outsourcing it with no strategy. You might hire a content writer to create blog posts and pay them $50 per weekly post. The problem is that these writers often work in a silo and lack focus. Their blog posts cover a random assortment of topics that may end up hurting you more than helping you. Even worse, a poorly-paid content writer might plagiarize content, which could get your website penalized. In short, regularly publishing content is good, but only if you have a clearly defined strategy. The strategy should take into consideration what content you've already published on your website and the gaps for attracting your target audience with new content.

Failure reason #3: Inconsistent efforts

The third mistake entrepreneurs often make is treating SEO like pay-per-click advertising, which can be turned on, completely changed, and turned off at a moment's notice. Unfortunately, SEO strategies require planning along with continuous efforts to publish targeted content while also applying strategies reviewed later in chapters 8 and 10 to increase the popularity of those pages with link building. If you start an SEO campaign and then abruptly stop, you lose all of the momentum you were building, and most of your content and investment will remain indexed on the fifth page of Google—or worse.

Failure reason #4: Hiring the wrong SEO experts

Lastly, SEO efforts can fail if you engage an SEO company that doesn't have experience working with your type of business and may deploy unproven strategies. If you're an e-commerce website, you don't want to work with a firm that specializes in only dentistry. You'll want to see that they have case studies in your profession and show proof that they work with businesses like yours.

A good strategy will be customized to your business's goals and will clearly lay out how they intend to increase traffic to your website using practices that have been effective for clients just like you. If the SEO company tries to sell you a generic bill of goods—a one-size-fits-all solution—their strategy will likely fail to produce results. A true, die-hard SEO expert will create a personalized strategy laid out in a spreadsheet that breaks down every aspect of your website's technical architecture. This includes content strategy and silos, URL structure, header tags, meta descriptions, internal link planning, structured markup, pillar pages, and more.

PLANNING YOUR PILLAR PAGES

At the top of your strategy checklist should be planning your pillar pages. A pillar page is a web page focused broadly on a single topic from which related in-depth pages—called "cluster content"—branch out. Pillar pages could range from 1,000–10,000 words, depending on how competitive that keyword or phrase is.

Using pillar pages is a good strategy that organizes your information by topic to make it easy for visitors to navigate and equally easy for Google to associate relevance while crawling and indexing. Remember, crawlability is a critical component to the success of your SEO campaign and site integrity, which can have a major impact on whether your site ranks high in search results or not.

To demonstrate how a pillar page works, imagine that you sell jeans. One pillar page you might want to create would be about different types of jeans. This page would then link to subtopic pages on your website that cover related topics and questions, such as "What is a bootcut jean," "What is a skinny jean," and "What is a straight-leg jean?" The pillar page would strategically and internally link to each of these subpages using keyword anchor text, such as bootcut jeans, to strengthen that content silo.

As another example, look at how Wikipedia structures its website. If you go to the Wikipedia page for baseball (the pillar page), you'll find a link to a subpage for batting. The batting page then introduces baserunners, and from baserunners you can link to a page about fielder's choice. This branching structure continues deeper and deeper to related content, but it all connects back to the pillar page for baseball and strengthens that content silo.

The goal is to build the most authoritative resource about a particular subject, which Wikipedia has been doing for years. This is no different from what you're trying to do with your website and digital marketing strategy.

A critical part of your content strategy will be deciding what pillar-page topics will help you connect with your target audience. Ask yourself these questions:

- What topics are important to your customers (or clients)?
- What questions are potential clients asking in Google searches?
- Who is already ranking on Google for these searches, and what does their content look like?
- What information does the user need to know?
- Do you have different geographic locations that need their own pages?
- What do the search volume and competition look like?

The benefit of preplanning your pillar pages and content strategy is that you can attract, inform, and educate targeted prospects who are looking for your specific product or service at the exact moment they want what you sell. You'll be able to measure your organic traffic for chosen keywords in Analytics after Google crawls and indexes your content. Then you can re-optimize your content to increase your rankings and traffic while growing your leads and revenue.

ORGANIC TRAFFIC

Organic traffic refers to the unpaid listings on a search engine results page (SERP) that the search engine has determined are most relevant to the user's query. You can't pay for your page to rank higher in organic search results.

STUDY YOUR COMPETITORS

To figure out what topics you want for your pillar pages, an excellent place to start is by studying your top competitors. If their websites are ranking at the top of Google searches, they're doing something right. There are insights and patterns on those pages that you or your content team can study when writing and publishing your content.

Your first step should be to find out who ranks at the top of Google searches for your market—they're your main SEO competition. Identifying your competition is as easy as searching what type of product or service you offer right in Google. If you're a "personal trainer in New York City," for example, run a search for that and see who comes up.

One thing to take into consideration is that the big spenders you recognize may not be using best practices with their technical SEO but may still be ranking. They've likely built up years of natural links from their advertising and community involvement, resulting in popularity superseding the technical aspects of their website. This goes to show how much weight Google places on links and popularity.

Don't be surprised to find that newer businesses in your niche are also top-ranking for some of these searches—this is where newcomers tend to have an advantage. People who have been in the market for a long time and have already built a brand may be susceptible to complacency, whereas a new kid on the block with a more sophisticated SEO strategy can swoop in and start to take away some of their online market share.

REVERSE ENGINEERING YOUR COMPETITORS' STRATEGIES

Once you have a list of your competitors, it's time to reverse engineer their SEO strategy. Start by crawling their websites using tools like Screaming Frog SEO Spider, Ahrefs, or Semrush (all of which I describe in greater detail in chapter 6).

KEYWORDS

Keywords are ideas and topics that define what your content is about. In terms of SEO, they're the words and phrases that searchers enter into search engines, also called "search queries."

These tools will provide insights and answer questions like "What keywords does the website rank for?" and "What does their backlink profile look like?" Also, pay attention to how the websites are technically structured, how pages link together, and how URLs are formatted. I suggest analyzing your top three competitors and making a spreadsheet with the following information:

- Number of total pages indexed on Google
- Number of organic keywords they are ranking for (using Semrush)
- Estimated organic traffic cost (Semrush)
- Estimated branded and non-branded traffic (Semrush)
- Domain rating, often abbreviated online and in SEO literature as DR (using Ahrefs)
- Total number of referring domains sorted by highest DR to lowest DR (Ahrefs)
- Top pages and all associated ranking keywords for each page (Ahrefs)

As you're studying your competitors' websites, compare them to your own. You want to set baseline metrics for measuring progress later. For example, look at how many pages Google has indexed on your website versus that of your competitors. You can do this by using the following search operator on a Google search:

site:yourdomain.com

By conducting this search on Google, it will report back how many pages it has indexed on your website. Do this same exercise for all of your competition to get a comparison. If you have 55 pages indexed on Google, and your largest competitor has 5,500 pages indexed on Google, then you may have some catching up to do.

When analyzing your website, you want to compare the number of HTML pages you have on your server versus the number of pages indexed on Google. If you have more pages indexed on Google, there might be some technical issues you need to fix, or you may have been hacked.

Barring a situation where you've been hacked, generally speaking, the more unique pages you have indexed on Google, the better. There are only two ways to increase organic traffic to a website from an SEO perspective: publishing more content that will rank for more keywords or pushing legacy pages higher in the SERPs with link-building strategies. For example, if you are ranking on the top of page two for a keyword that has 5,000 searches per month, pushing it to the first page of Google would increase your impressions, click-throughs, and traffic.

Creating the high-level blueprint for your strategy might not be as exciting as designing the look and feel of your website, but it's as necessary as the first step of architecting a building before breaking ground. If you put in the time now to plan your pillar pages, study the competition, set baseline metrics and goals, and reverse engineer winning strategies, you'll set yourself up for long-term SEO success.

→ Create your personalized SEO strategy blueprint before building your website (or redesigning it).

→ Plan out your pillar pages and the more in-depth subpages that will link to them.

→ Identify the top competitors in your market.

→ Study your competitors' websites using tools like Screaming Frog SEO Spider, Ahrefs, and Semrush. Pay attention to their content strategy, ranking keywords, backlinks, and more.

→ Reverse engineer your competitors' strategies so you can dominate your market and take more digital market share.

CHAPTER 5

Your Digital Marketing Team

You now understand the basics of SEO and have begun to draft a high-level strategy that will help boost your website's search ranking and start generating more profit for your business. You can get the ball rolling yourself, but your passion probably isn't building links—it's building and growing your business. Your time is better spent doing what you do best. This means your next step is hiring a team (even if you can afford only two people) to develop and execute the SEO strategy.

You've reached a fork in the road. As we mention in the previous section, if you have a lot of time and a lot of technical skills and interest, you can do some of this on your own. But there's a limit to what you can achieve, and even if you do have a lot of time and a lot of interest in the subject of SEO, I *strongly* suggest you hire a team. So who do you hire? How big is the team? And how do you make these decisions in the first place?

These are the questions this chapter answers. No matter which path you choose, you'll also need to know how to hold your digital marketing team accountable. So many entrepreneurs have been burned by the agency or so-called specialist they hired to manage their SEO.

They may charge thousands of dollars a month and yet fail to deliver results—but that cycle ends now.

By the time you're finished with this chapter, you'll know:

- Whether you need an in-house team or an external agency
- The job titles and competencies you want for your digital marketing team
- How to write a compelling job description that attracts top talent
- How to define and measure success

THE MINIMUM VIABLE TEAM FOR A SMALL BUSINESS

SEO isn't just one thing. It requires a lot of different skill sets. No one person is good at everything. That's why we hire people—to help us out on the things that aren't in our particular zones of genius.

But you might be financially strapped. If that's the case, hire as many in-house team members as financially possible. At the end of the day, only you can realistically look at your situation and make that call.

Conversely, you might still be wondering how (and if) you can do this all on your own. I understand; in the beginning, I did a lot of the work on my own, too.

At first, it usually starts with a curiosity about the subject. Maybe you go to the bookstore and pick up a book or two on SEO. Maybe you're reading more about SEO, and eventually, you're hooked. Eventually, you start familiarizing yourself with WordPress, and you're publishing more and more content. At some point, though, you'll realize that everything you're doing isn't the best use of your time. Even starting out on your own, all roads eventually lead to hiring.

And there's another complication. Depending on the competition you're facing, with a small team you might not be able to do enough to make a difference. If the keywords you're competing for have a lot of competition and the only person working on the SEO is you, you most likely won't be able to outrank them.

With these caveats in mind, then, for the cash-strapped entrepreneur, the most minimum viable team is two people:

- A writer
- A technical expert

What would this look like in practice? At first, as I mention earlier, try to find out how prospects find you on Google. Do a little keyword research yourself. For the business you're in, what does the market share look like? What are your prospects typing in the Google search bar to search for products or services similar to what you offer?

From there, develop a blueprint for your website (see chapter 4). Don't hire a designer or anyone just yet. First, simply build the blueprint of your website and, using your keyword research, figure out what pages are on the website, what the website looks like, and what the blog looks like. From there, once you have a blueprint, you'll identify the roles you need.

First, I'd recommend a content writer. Then hire a technical expert, someone who can make sure the backend of your website is helping, not hurting, your SEO. From there, you can add on. Maybe you hire a graphic designer, then a PR specialist. As your business begins to do better, you can hire more and more people.

Make sure the foundation is set before you hire. First, create the blueprint, then hire people to build your house.

WHAT IF YOU'RE A MEDIUM-SIZED BUSINESS?

The progression we've just discussed wouldn't make sense if you're a medium-sized business because you have other, more cost-effective options, depending on where your website is currently ranking.

If you're a medium-sized business, then you have essentially two options. You can choose to build an in-house SEO team or hire an agency. Building an in-house SEO team has many benefits, including control over your data, over whom you choose to hire, and over which person does what job, among other considerations. However, unless your company does a volume of business that justifies spending upward of $25,000 per month on an in-house marketing team, you'll likely be better served by hiring an outside agency.

"Now, hold on, Jason," you might be thinking. "Why can't I hire one salaried SEO specialist for $70,000 a year to do all the work?"

As I mention above, a single person won't have all the proficiencies and array of talents needed to do an exceptional job. You wouldn't hire one person to build your house—you'd hire an architect, an electrician, a plumber, and so on. You shouldn't hire a single person to manage and execute your overall SEO strategy.

In the case of a small business, hiring one or two people can make sense, but only because of the aforementioned reasons: you don't have enough cash to hire more, and you're competing for less sought-after keywords. The reality for a medium-sized business is that the keywords are more competitive, and they're competing on a different level. Remember: your strength on Google only matters to the degree that you can beat out competitors. There's a difference between competing for "running shoes" versus "orthopedic shoes for children," so keep scale in mind.

A good digital marketing agency will have people who specialize in all the areas you need, and for their monthly fee (five figures is reasonable for a mid-sized business), you'll have access to them all. That price tag might sound expensive until you consider the astronomically higher cost of hiring all those specialists separately, building the strategy yourself, and then managing them. For these reasons, working with a reputable agency that has a large team and a proven strategy is often the best choice for most businesses. It keeps costs reasonable while still granting you access to top talent who are experts in their fields, not to mention the savings of thousands of dollars in licenses and tools that are necessary to develop, monitor, and execute the strategy.

A word of warning: if an agency gives you a low quote—let's say $1,500 per month—that might be a red flag. There's no way the agency can devote enough resources to your SEO to make a difference and still make a profit for such a low cost. Think about all of the SEO efforts I discussed so far in this book, and now consider how many hours that $1,500 will get you. Heck, I even pay interns more than that at my agency. The time required and the time afforded do not add up with such a low budget and will most likely not produce results.

Here's what tends to happen with cheap agencies: several months may pass with little to no results. The business hiring the agency typically gets frustrated and puts pressure on the agency to start producing return on investment (ROI). The agency, still with too few resources to make a real impact, might take shortcuts, perhaps even turning to black hat SEO strategies to show short-term gains.

Before long, Google catches on to these tactics, which may go against Google's webmaster guidelines, and penalize your website. In this way, opting for a cheap agency may not only fail to produce results, but it can actually do more harm than good. And this, my friends, is why SEO agencies have such a bad rep. Welcome to my world!

KEY ROLES ON A DIGITAL MARKETING TEAM

Whether you're starting out with a minimum viable team, hiring an agency, or building your own in-house digital marketing team, it's important to know which roles should be present. What does the perfect in-house or agency digital marketing team look like, and why does it look that way?

A strong digital marketing team should include the following roles:

- Marketing director
- Digital marketing manager
- Copywriter
- Technical SEO lead
- Web developer
- Public relations specialist
- Link-building and outreach specialist

- Social media manager

- Paid media strategist

- Graphic designer

- Video editor

- Data analyst

Let's go through each role from the perspective of hiring a digital marketing team.

Marketing director

Your company might be investing in digital marketing while also doing community outreach, advertising on the radio, and putting up billboards in your city, and someone needs to be the ringleader of these activities. That person is a marketing director—the individual who oversees and coordinates all of your various marketing efforts while budgeting, tracking, and attributing your return on ad spend for each marketing channel.

Suppose you hire an external digital marketing agency. In that case, you might have a marketing director on your staff who manages the relationship with your digital marketing agency directly or manages an internal digital marketing manager who works with the agency and holds them accountable.

Digital marketing manager

The digital marketing manager, as the name suggests, focuses solely on your digital efforts. This person is the liaison between the digital marketing team and your company's marketing director, and they also manage the other roles on the digital marketing team.

Larger businesses might have a digital marketing manager on staff who specializes in specific tactics such as pay-per-click advertising but not SEO. In this case, they consider working with an SEO agency because SEO is not their core competency. The digital marketing manager would be responsible for attending meetings with the agency, reviewing the content they produce, and generally making sure the agency produces results.

Copywriter

The new web pages you'll create will need clear, well-presented information that speaks to your target audience, and the person with the skill set to do that is a copywriter. While their job title is "copywriter," you ideally want someone whose talents also include storytelling, or you'll want to hire two people with different skill sets.

The most compelling websites do more than regurgitate dry facts. They tell a story in a way that your potential customers can relate to, and the copywriter is responsible for telling the story of your business. In shaping that story, think about the problems you solve for your target audience and the challenges they have faced. What was your role in their success?

Too many companies simply *say* what they do without actually addressing how their potential customers feel and think. A good copywriter will capture this emotion and be able to tell a compelling story about your business's mission while using empathy to appeal to the psyche of the user.

Technical SEO lead

On any SEO team, you'll also want to have someone who specializes in technical issues. They're the person who will fix PageSpeed problems, develop internal linking strategies, optimize content and source code using schema markup, and monitor tools like Google Search Console to continuously identify and fix all technical errors. It's important that the technical SEO lead is proactive and not reactive with your overall strategy. They should look for new opportunities to leverage your web assets while increasing your rankings and traffic. They will also be your go-to when Google releases an algorithmic update that shakes up the SERPs.

GOOGLE SEARCH CONSOLE

Google Search Console is a free service offered by Google that helps you monitor, maintain, and troubleshoot your site's presence in Google search results.

According to Google, Search Console offers tools and reports for the following actions:

- Confirm that Google can find and crawl your site

- Fix indexing problems and request re-indexing of new or updated content

- View Google search traffic data for your site: how often your site appears in Google search, which search queries show your site, how often searchers click through for those queries, and more

- Receive alerts when Google encounters indexing, spam, or other issues on your site

- Show you which sites link to your website

- Troubleshoot issues for AMP, mobile usability, and other search features

Web developer

The web developer works on the website to implement the recommendations of the technical SEO lead. They typically have HTML, CSS, PHP, JavaScript, and WordPress experience. I recommend avoiding platforms like Wix and Squarespace for your website because they give you less control over your website's functionality, which may impede your efforts when you want to use more advanced SEO practices. The web developer should also know how to speed up the performance, handle backend programming, deal with the server, fix broken links, and eliminate unnecessary redirects, among other website responsibilities.

Public relations specialist

The public relations specialist interacts with the media and builds relationships with reporters, writers, and publications. They build your company's public image as a subject-matter expert, set up speaking engagements, arrange podcast opportunities, and pitch you for contributor columns on sites like *Forbes, Inc.*, and *Entrepreneur*. It's important for the public relations specialist to be able to work with the media on different story angles, land featured articles, and get quotes placed with reputable media platforms, including online, print, podcasts, television, and more. We cover this in more detail in chapter 9.

Link-building and outreach specialist

Your digital marketing team should also include someone responsible for outreach and link building. They'll perform some of the reverse-engineering work discussed in the previous chapter to ensure that your website has as many or more quality links as your competitors. They'll strategically add your business to directories and coordinate with the copywriter to distribute press releases that generate news links. They will also build relationships with bloggers for guest blog post opportunities and work with the copywriter to create assets they can use in their outreach initiatives to attract more links and boost the authority of the website.

Social media manager

A strong digital marketing team will also have a social media manager who handles all organic social media growth. This is one role that benefits from being part of your internal team instead of part of the agency you hire, and that's because social media engagement requires an in-office presence. You want someone who understands the market and can capture the essence of life at your business, interact with clients or customers, understand your culture, and create engagement with your followers. While you can hire an agency to help develop a strategy, in my experience, this position makes more sense to have someone who works in-house.

Paid media strategist

The paid media strategist has a different skill set than the social media manager in that they work with paid ad campaigns, not organic social activity. They know how to build pay-per-click campaigns on Google, Bing, YouTube, and other search engines. The paid media strategist also sets up paid campaigns and retargeting campaigns on Facebook and other social media channels. They should understand how to modify campaigns on a daily basis to maximize impact and the cost per converted customer, so you know exactly what you're getting for your paid media budget.

Graphic designer

Text only makes up part of your website's content, which is why you'll also want a graphic designer on the team. This person might be an employee of the digital marketing agency or a freelancer. Chances are you'll need their services more than you expect. Regularly publishing content requires graphics for blog posts, social media, infographics, pillar pages, subtopic pages, and even YouTube thumbnails.

Video editor

Video is more prevalent and effective at generating leads than ever before, so having a video editor on hand is as important as a graphic designer. Occasionally, these two skill sets overlap, but you might need to hire individuals for each role. You'll want to publish videos to YouTube as well as other video-hosting websites because each instance counts as a link pointing back to your website. Plus, having video on the top of your important pages will keep people on the page longer and increase the chances of converting that traffic to leads.

Data analyst

Lastly, your team should have a data analyst in charge of tracking data and making sure leads get attributed to the right sources. If your company spends money on both pay-per-click ads and SEO, you need a way to discern which efforts are producing results. Are you getting more leads from pay-per-click or from SEO?

You won't know what works without data, so your analyst plays a critical role in gauging the effectiveness of your overall digital marketing investment. The analyst defines and measures success, handles conversion rate optimization, runs split tests to compare different design options, and creates the reports that keep you apprised of progress and your return on investment.

THE RIGHT TEAM FOR YOUR BUSINESS

Choosing whether to build your own digital marketing team or hire an agency is a big decision, but again, for most small businesses, going with an agency will most likely be the best economical and effective solution. Generally speaking, for the same price it would take to hire just a single competent member of an in-house team, you gain access to the full expertise of an agency with dozens or more professionals who are experts in their fields.

At the very least, you'll want this hired digital marketing team to perform the roles described in the previous section. Some of these roles might overlap—for example, it's possible (but rare) to find someone who's knowledgeable in both technical SEO and web development. In most cases, these are very different skill sets. The important thing to remember is that both of these skill sets should be represented on your digital marketing team.

To make sure you're hiring the right agency for your business, do your due diligence. Start with the following actions:

- Ask the agency if they work with other businesses like yours and understand the marketing space you're in.

- Use the tools I mention in earlier chapters to see if their SEO has been effective with previous clients.

- Speak with their references.

- Ask to speak to the last business that fired them. It's interesting to see how they answer that question.

- Ask what roles the team will include and who does what. Ensure they have most of the talent and skills previously mentioned in this chapter.

- Does the agency have a graphic designer? Is someone proficient in technical SEO? What does their content team look like? Do they even have a content team? You'd be surprised; there are many agencies that don't offer copywriting as a service.

- Ask them to send examples of their work. Read the examples, and then ask yourself if you would feel comfortable patronizing the business for which they wrote the copy—after all, you want their copy to make potential customers comfortable doing business with you.

Unscrupulous SEO companies may be counting on the fact that most entrepreneurs don't understand SEO and how it works. But now, you're armed with the knowledge you need to never be taken advantage of again.

LOOK FOR TALENT BEYOND YOUR BACKYARD

Once upon a time, working as a team meant gathering in the same office every day. The necessity of physical proximity limited your hiring choices to only the people willing to make the commute. Being headquartered in a small town also meant a small talent pool. But those days are over.

With virtual technology and video chats, you can hire digital marketing professionals from anywhere in the country or even the world. There's no reason to limit yourself to local talent when you could have a marketing director in one state and a graphic designer in another. In fact, that's how I've built my agency. My team works together remotely with over 100 people collaborating from around the globe.

In this way, technology has allowed us to recruit some of the smartest minds in digital marketing regardless of where they are located.

HOLDING YOUR TEAM ACCOUNTABLE

Once you've found the right digital marketing team, your next challenge will be to hold them accountable. Your ability to hold people accountable depends entirely on you being aware of what they're doing and understanding the outcomes. Ask yourself the following questions:

- Is the digital marketing team publishing content on a regular basis?
- Am I satisfied with the content they're putting out?
- If I were a potential lead, would I be sold on what my business offers based on what I'm seeing?

If the answer to any of these questions is no, you probably want to make adjustments quickly before they continue to go down this path for months on end. The most successful businesses marketing online have somebody working closely with the marketing team and providing feedback. The team is only going to be as successful as your engagement with them is. You might consider giving this book to your director of marketing so they can hold their team or agency accountable.

As you guide your digital marketing team's efforts, always focus on putting your customers and potential customers first. If you aren't getting results, the problem might not be your team's actions but the direction and subject of the content itself. Start by stepping into your customers' or clients' shoes. Your website should answer the questions they might have. In other words, try to separate yourself from what you already know and instead think about what your *customers* need to know. These are the topics and questions you want to address that will boost your traffic and increase the number of potential customers buying what you offer.

•

Remember, you are not writing to entice someone exactly like you. When writing your content, I recommend expressing an understanding of what your reader might be feeling and writing at an 8th-grade reading level. You want to write a response that you'd want to receive if you were in that circumstance.

YOU CAN'T CONTROL WHAT YOU DON'T UNDERSTAND

Remember that SEO is like trying to turn the grass in your yard green. You can control certain inputs, like how much you water the grass and whether you put down fertilizer, but you can't control the sun. In the same way, you can control your SEO inputs like link building and content creation, but you can't control Google's algorithm. However, both the sun and Google's algorithm are unpredictable.

And here's one more key part to the equation: to determine if your yard care is working, you need to monitor the grass and understand whether it's improving or dying. It's the same with SEO.

When you understand what work your digital marketing team is doing and why they're doing it, you can also understand and predict their results. You can compare those results to the baseline to determine whether your team has been successful, and in doing so, you can hold them accountable. You can't measure what you don't understand, so choosing the right team for your business and understanding their efforts are critical to seeing positive SEO outcomes.

→ You have the option to either build your own in-house digital marketing team or hire an outside agency.

→ If you're cash-strapped, you can hire a minimum viable team with the intention of growing in the future.

→ For most businesses, it probably makes financial sense to hire an agency. You can pay much less than it would cost to build an in-house team, and you'll still have access to a wide range of experts in their specific fields.

→ A great SEO team needs people to write content, manage technical SEO aspects, and analyze the results.

→ Your digital marketing team should include the following roles: marketing director, digital marketing manager, copywriter, technical SEO lead, web developer, public relations specialist, link-building and outreach specialist, social media manager, paid media strategist, graphic designer, video editor, and data analyst.

→ Once you've hired your team, hold them accountable. You can't control what you don't understand, so it's important to follow the reports, review their work yourself, and monitor progress over time.

SEO

TOOLS

CHAPTER 6

Tools to Help You Measure Success

In the same way you can't know that your grass is getting greener without looking at it, you won't know if your SEO efforts are working without measuring the results. Whether you've decided to tackle your own SEO, hire an in-house person, or hire an agency, you need the tools I describe in this chapter.

These tools can provide insights on website performance, site integrity, keyword research, content strategy, link analysis, traffic monitoring, and more. All of these will give you a deeper understanding of how Google evaluates your website and indexes it within the search engine results pages (SERPs).

GOOGLE IS YOUR MOST POWERFUL TOOL

Dozens of tools exist to help you organize your SEO activity, measure performance, and manage your website, but perhaps the strongest tool of all is Google itself.

Search operators

One of the most powerful tools for finding the information you need on Google is the search operator. Google allows you to use short commands called "search operators" to refine your search queries so you can find exactly what you're looking for. They are commands that tell Google how to include, exclude, and sort its data.

Here are a few examples of the most useful operators.

Site:

The **site**: search operator will give you a lot of useful insights when analyzing your website against your competition. Not only will this reveal how many pages of content your website has indexed on Google, but it will also help you forensically audit technical issues with your site. This is where SEO starts to become fun. As we discuss in chapter 4, here's a useful tool. Go to Google, type this command into the search bar, and press enter:

site:yourdomain.com

After the results populate, you should see the word "About" with a number next to it. This is a good estimate of the number of pages your domain has indexed on Google. Now do the same exercise using your competitors' websites. If they have 5,000 pages of content indexed and you only have 270 indexed, you may need to keep working at content creation to catch up.

The **site**: search operator is also a clever way to look for technical problems and opportunities on your website forensically. For example, if you do a **site:yourdomain.com** search on Google and find that there are 10,000 pages of content indexed but you know you should have only a few hundred pages, then you have either been hacked or there could be other technical problems that need to be addressed. This is one case where more is not necessarily better. Google may think you have a bunch of duplicate pages on your site.

Here are just a few more ways to use the **site**: search operator to your benefit:

site:yourdomain.com -inurl:https

This search operator will help you audit your HTTP to HTTPS transition and discover any old HTTP pages that might not have been re-crawled by Google. (The hyphen is part of the command.)

Here is another way to learn about indexing on your website, though you'll want to tailor it to your own industry specifics.

site:yourdomain.com intitle:orthopedic tennis shoes

This search operator will show you all of the pages on your site that are indexed and optimized for the keyword "orthopedic tennis shoes" within your title tag, revealing internal linking opportunities or cannibalization problems (which we explore in chapter 10). You can replace "orthopedic tennis shoes" with any keyword of your choice.

TITLE TAG

The **title tag** is an HTML code tag that allows you to give a web page a title. This title can be found in the browser title bar, as well as in the search engine results pages (SERPs). It's crucial to add and optimize your website's title tags, as they play an essential role in terms of organic ranking (SEO).

Cache:

The **cache**: search operator will return the most recently cached version of a web page (provided the page is indexed, of course). This operator is different from the rest; instead of searching for it in Google like the others, you enter this command in your address bar, and press enter:

cache:yourdomain.com

You need to be using Chrome as your browser or Google as the major search engine for it to work. This is a great way to see how often Google crawls and indexes your content. You can also use this search operator to confirm that pages with valuable links are cached and indexed. If not, you can use different pinging techniques to get Google to cache and index the page so they see and follow the link passing both PageRank and TrustRank. These are ranking systems that are scored on a scale of 0 to 10. The higher the scores, the more authoritative and trustworthy the site.

PINGING, PAGERANK, AND TRUSTRANK

Pinging consists of submitting new pages so that the search engine robots can index them and, as a result, increase their visibility in the search results. Simply put, the pinging process itself is nothing more than informing the search engine crawlers that new content has appeared on a website.

PageRank (PR) is an algorithm used by Google search to rank web pages in their search engine results. It is named after both the term "web page" and co-founder Larry Page. PageRank is a way of measuring the importance of website pages.

TrustRank is an algorithm that conducts link analysis to separate useful web pages from spam and helps search engine rank pages in SERPs (search engine results pages). It is a semiautomated process, which means that it needs some human assistance in order to function properly. Search engines have many different algorithms and ranking factors that they use when measuring the quality of web pages. TrustRank is one of them.

TrustRank is an algorithm that conducts link analysis to separate reputable web pages from spam. In other words, Google up-ranks websites that it trusts, and they measure that trust in their algorithm with TrustRank. The closer a site is to spam resources, the more likely it is to be spam as well. That is why it is important to be careful about which sites you link out to and monitor which sites link back to your website.

Find people who are stealing your content

Copy a snippet of content from any page on your website. Then, take that snippet and conduct a Google search using quotation marks around the snippet. Follow that with this designator:

-site:yourdomain.com

By using the **"snippet of text from your web page"** **-site:yourdomain.com** search operator, Google will search for the exact phrase in your copy text and exclude any pages from your website in the search results. If Google doesn't return anything, that is a good thing. However, if Google returns results with other businesses or websites that have the same exact content, you might have a duplicate-content problem that needs to be addressed.

Find guest post link-building opportunities

Use the search operator as a link-building tool to find websites that accept guest blog posts. Go to Google, enter any of these search queries into the search bar, and press enter. You will find thousands of link opportunities.

"[your keyword]" + "write for us"

"[your keyword]" + "write for me"

"[your keyword]" + "become a contributor"

"[your keyword]" + "guest post"

"[your keyword]" + "contribute"

"[your keyword]" + "submit a guest post"

"[your keyword]" + "accepting guest posts"

If you specialized in personal finance for freelancers, you could use **"[personal finance]" + "write for us"** or **"[freelancers]" + "guest post"**.

Using search operators will help you refine your search queries much more efficiently than using Google's normal search.

Please keep in mind that we only touched on a few of the basic search operators, but their uses can get much more advanced. If you are looking for all of the ways you can leverage advanced search operators, I highly recommend reading the book *Google Power Search*, written by a good friend and colleague of mine, Stephan Spencer. It's one of the books I keep at my desk at all times, and I reference it often when doing technical site audits or research projects.

"People Also Ask"

Another useful functionality of Google is its "People Also Ask" feature. By searching for a keyword or question, Google will most likely provide you with FAQs related to your initial search query. If you click the last question, then more questions will continue to populate. These questions can be an excellent source of content topics as you build out your content strategy, which includes pillar pages and subtopics that speak to your audience's needs.

For example, if I type "Chicago yoga class" into Google's search bar, it might return the following questions:

- What are people saying about yoga in Chicago, IL?
- What are some highly rated yoga studios in Chicago, IL?
- How expensive are yoga classes in Chicago, IL?

If you own a yoga studio in Chicago, these are questions that your target audience might be asking. By creating a content strategy that provides answers to these questions in the form of text, video, or both, you'll get more targeted traffic to your website and increase your chances of converting that visitor into a client.

PageSpeed Insights

Another free tool that can help you measure your website's performance is Google's PageSpeed Insights.

In the PageSpeed Insights search bar, simply type in your website's URL and click "analyze." It will return a score from 0 to 100 for both the desktop and mobile version of your site. It's important to note that these scores are different, and both should be taken seriously. All too often, people will only focus on their desktop PageSpeed and not realize there's a different mobile score as well, and they'll wonder why their SEO strategy is not working. Think about this from Google's perspective: a user conducts a search, finds your page indexed, and clicks on it, only for it to take 17 seconds to load. This creates a bad user experience for Google's client, which is why Google takes PageSpeed so seriously. Bottom line: the faster and more reliable your web page, the better chances you have of ranking higher on Google.

Not only will this tool give you a speed score, but it will also provide detailed technical suggestions for increasing your score and making that page faster. For example, the tool might suggest removing unnecessary scripts, compressing large images, fixing JavaScript problems, and a bunch of other technical jargon that you don't necessarily need to understand. The beautiful thing about this tool is that you, as a novice, only need to know how to put your URL in the tool and press enter. Continue to run the tool and follow their technical instructions until you score 90 percent or higher on both mobile and desktop.

This is a great way to hold your technical SEO lead and web developer accountable. In fact, this is so important that I suggest you take a break from reading this book and go conduct this experiment now. Please note that if you have scripts running on your site like Google Analytics, web chat, Facebook, or others, that will most likely lower your score.

Google Search Console

Google Search Console, another free tool, provides utilities and reports that measure your website's performance and identify technical problems. Google Search Console is in a league of its own because it's the only platform that allows you to have a two-way conversation with Google.

When Google identifies a problem with your website, you will be alerted through an email from Google and can take specific action to fix the issues. There are so many benefits to this tool, but I'd be willing to bet that six out of ten people reading this book don't even know that it exists. This tool is how Google alerts you about manual actions and penalties and provides you with a means to file a reconsideration request if your site gets penalized. It allows you to monitor, maintain, and troubleshoot your site's presence in Google's search results. Furthermore, it proactively or reactively guards against negative SEO attacks by way of disavowing bad backlinks. We talk more about negative SEO in chapter 13.

DISAVOW BACKLINKS

Disavow Backlinks is a tool in Search Console which allows you to request that Google not take certain spammy links into account when assessing your site.

Like the other tools in this chapter, the insights gained from Search Console will give you a competitive advantage for ranking higher on Google if you proactively fix all technical blockers reported. Without this tool, you are flying blind and left guessing why your SEO is not performing. So again, put down the book, grab some coffee, and text whoever is currently responsible for your digital marketing strategy to make sure that you have this tool connected to your site.

Google Analytics

Google Analytics is another free tool that needs to be in your SEO toolbox. It is used to track website activity such as session duration, pages per session, bounce rate, and tracking conversions and goals, among other things. Unlike Google Search Console, which provides leading indicators such as technical improvements that you can make to your website, Google Analytics shows you whether those improvements made a difference. It does this by providing you with lagging indicators of increased traffic, more time spent on your page, and your conversion percentages. In addition, because it's a Google tool, Analytics has direct access to search data and information from other Google products that third-party tools lack.

THIRD-PARTY SEO TOOLS

As you can see, Google itself is one of the most powerful tools at your disposal. Google provides you with many other free services, but plenty of valuable third-party software and applications exist to fill in the gaps. Here's an overview of different tools that should absolutely be in your SEO arsenal.

Ahrefs

Ahrefs is a comprehensive, all-in-one SEO software suite that contains tools for link-building analysis, keyword research, rank tracking, site audits, and reverse engineering your competitors' SEO strategies. If I had to pick just a few paid tools that I highly recommend, Ahrefs would absolutely be one of them. In fact, I probably spend at least two hours per day using this tool.

What it does:

- Backlink analysis
- Keyword research
- Content gap analysis
- Technical site auditing
- Competitive analysis
- Rank tracking

Where to find it: **ahrefs.com**

Semrush

Like Ahrefs, Semrush is an all-in-one tool suite for improving online visibility and discovering digital marketing insights. They have an easy-to-use interface that can help you with your organic research, domain overview comparisons, link analysis, social media audits, and pay-per-click tools. It even possesses content marketing templates that will help you write and optimize your web copy to rank higher on Google. This is the other paid tool that is essential for your SEO and digital marketing success. In fact, if you polled a roomful of SEO experts, I'd be willing to bet that nearly all of them use both Ahrefs and Semrush.

What it does:

- Runs a technical SEO audit of your site (or any other URL)
- Tracks your daily rankings
- Analyzes your competitors' SEO strategies
- Analyzes the backlink profile of any domain
- Provides relevant keyword ideas

Where to find it: **semrush.com**

Screaming Frog SEO Spider

Screaming Frog SEO Spider is a "spider tool" that crawls websites in the same way Google does. It identifies technical blockers and extracts data for your SEO team to analyze and fix problems in real time. Unlike the tools mentioned above, Screaming Frog is a program that you download and run on your own computer.

What it does:

- Finds broken links
- Audits redirects
- Analyzes page titles and metadata
- Finds duplicate content and identifies cannibalization problems
- Generates XML sitemaps

Where to find it: **screamingfrog.co.uk**

Copyscape

Copyscape is a plagiarism checker that can detect duplicate content on the web. It checks for plagiarism on your website, which is important if you're buying articles or other content from freelancers, and it checks for *your* content on other websites so you can tell if anyone has stolen from you. Duplicate content can negatively affect your entire strategy, so it's important to deal with it quickly when it's found.

What it does:

- Checks your website for plagiarized content (you want to make sure writers aren't selling you duplicate content)
- Searches the web for stolen instances of your original content
- Sends you an email notification when it finds plagiarized content

Where to find it: **copyscape.com**

Siteliner

Siteliner is a service that scans your website and reveals internal duplicate content problems. Having multiple pages with similar content on your website can confuse Google and negatively affect your search rankings.

What it does:

- Identifies internal duplicate content
- Finds broken links
- Analyzes pages to reveal which are most prominent to search engines
- Provides reports on page optimization

Where to find it: **siteliner.com**

BrightLocal

BrightLocal is an integrated local SEO and citation platform that offers cost-effective aggregator submissions and a citation-building service to help increase your local rankings. BrightLocal also offers reputation and review management tools, local SEO audits, and an interactive dashboard with lots of useful data and metrics.

What it does:

- Tracks local rankings
- Audits and builds citations
- Reports on local SEO
- Reports and offers tools on multiple locations
- Manages reputation and reviews

Where to find it: **brightlocal.com**

Podium

Podium, a Google-backed venture, is a messaging platform that allows you to communicate more easily with clients and leads. For example, you might use Podium to text customers or leads and ask them to leave a review on your Google Business Profile listing or Yelp.

What it does:

- Manages reviews and allows you to communicate with customers online
- Makes it easy to send standardized text messages
- Shows you competitive benchmarks for star rating, review count, and more

Where to find it: **podium.com**

UserWay

UserWay is an automated accessibility solution that will help make your website more compatible with the Americans with Disabilities Act (ADA) and Web Content Accessibility Guidelines (WCAG) requirements.

What it does:

- Enables user-triggered accessibility enhancements on your site
- Changes text size, font, contrast, and other formatting and design elements to be accessible
- Reads text aloud
- Moderates offensive content
- Reduces your liability to potential lawsuits

Where to find it: **userway.org**

THE SEO JOB REQUIRES THE RIGHT TOOLS

It might seem like a hassle to juggle so many different tools at once, but make no mistake, SEO tools are essential for success. A dentist wouldn't fix a cavity with their bare hands, and a contractor wouldn't build a house without a hammer. An SEO practitioner won't have much effect without their tool set.

Without insights and data, there's no way to know if your strategy is working, so you absolutely must track where you started, where your performance is now, and where you plan to go with your digital marketing goals to grow revenue and sign more cases.

TIPS AND TAKEAWAYS: SEO TOOLS

→ Google itself offers some of the most powerful tools in SEO: search operators, "People Also Ask" (frequently asked questions), PageSpeed Insights, Google Search Console, and Google Analytics.

→ Many third-party tools are available for link analysis, keyword research, conversion rate optimization (CRO), online visibility, technical SEO audits, internal and external duplicate content problems, and every other area where you might need additional insight and guidance.

→ While there may be a lot to learn and manage, these tools play a critical role in the success of your digital marketing strategy.

CONTENT

STRATEGY

CHAPTER 7

Content Strategy

Google is nothing if not a tool to search through the vast amounts of content created by other people. Without content, Google would not exist. This is why developing your content strategy is perhaps the most important part of your SEO efforts.

I've already talked about your high-level SEO game plan, but now it's time to dig deeper into the planning, development, and management of your content strategy. People often make the mistake of simply hiring a content writer to churn out articles without any guidance, structure, or information architecture. Even large companies that have been in business for years may be guilty of this approach.

For your content efforts to produce a meaningful increase in website traffic from your target audience, the content must be focused, positioned to outrank your competitors' content, tailored to your audience, and aligned with your overall SEO strategy.

WHAT IS CONTENT?

Content comes in many shapes and forms, including text copy, infographics, and video. Depending on your business, you'll have different content pages. Here are a few ideas for content pages you might want on your website:

- Frequently asked questions (FAQs)
- Information about your business and the types of customers you service
- "About Us" page for your business
- Bios for your team members
- Contact information
- Testimonials from happy customers
- News, events, and press releases
- Community involvement
- Career opportunities
- Engaging social media posts
- Blog (only if you're prepared to post regularly; a neglected blog reflects poorly on your business)

These are just a few of the different content pages you'll likely want to include in your strategy. Content encompasses all the information that lives on your website, but for the purposes of this chapter and the strategy you'll create, I speak primarily about text on a page.

WHO IS YOUR AUDIENCE?

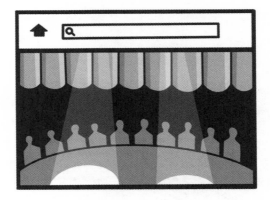

The first question you should ask yourself in shaping your content strategy is "Who is your target audience?"

You want to attract more potential leads to your website, but who, specifically, will be the most profitable leads for your business? What is their demographic? What problems do they have? Why do they need you and the solutions you offer?

As part of this exploration process, you'll want to use the keyword research tools introduced in the last chapter to identify terms and phrases your audience is searching for. You'll also want to turn to the research you've done in reverse engineering your competitors' content strategies. However, looking at your competitors is not enough on its own. Instead, aim to learn from their strategies while staying within your own area of expertise.

By this, I don't simply mean that you should copy their content. For example, if a competitor specializes in renting out camera equipment whereas your business focuses on selling camera equipment, building out your content strategy around camera rentals is the wrong approach. Instead, make it your goal to take market share in the areas and audiences where you will excel based on your professional experience. Decide who your audience is, and build a content strategy that speaks to them.

WHERE IS YOUR AUDIENCE?

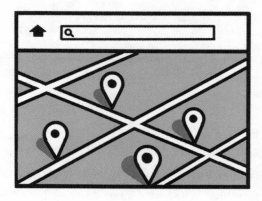

Once you've thought about *who* your audience is, you must cater to *where* they are.

The most effective way to reach your target audience is to create content specifically for where your audience lives. If you're a financial professional who serves clients in Malibu, California, you need to create a web page optimized for that geographic location. This guideline especially applies to areas where you don't have a physical location because you don't have the advantage of appearing on Google Maps. You need to insert yourself into that market by having a targeted page optimized for that specific location and practice area.

When a user searches for "financial adviser" on Google, Google automatically knows where they're located and assumes they're looking for a professional in their area. That means if you don't have a page optimized for Malibu, a competitor who *does* have that geographic-specific page will outrank you in the search results.

If you're thinking, "This seems redundant. Are you saying I need to create content for every small area in my market," the answer is yes.

As people perform searches for general phrases like "help with taxes" and "investing advice" without typing a city name, Google tailors the search results to their location based on their IP address. Again, if you're not listed on Google Maps for those locations because you don't have a brick-and-mortar office, it is next to impossible to rank on Google for these terms. The only way to rank within those areas, short of having an office location in every market you wish to serve, is by having pages explicitly optimized for those areas at the town or city level.

As an example, imagine you're an IT professional based in Santa Clarita, California, but you also serve clients in Santa Monica, Burbank, and Los Angeles. You might want to have a web page that uses a title tag optimized for "IT Professional in Santa Clarita, CA." On this page, the copy would express some empathy about their frustration with the technical side of running the business, typically in the first two paragraphs, and include information about the consequences they're facing in lost time and lost efficiency. You would also share information about how you can help and how they can contact you. You'd want to make this page hyper-relevant to Santa Clarita by referencing the local companies you've worked with and creating external links to connect your web page with local businesses. This is important because it allows Google to associate your web page with authoritative and trusted resources by way of a link and citation.

Next, you'd want to create similar pages for each geographic location you serve, such as "IT Professional in Santa Monica, CA," and "IT Professional in Burbank, CA." You would swap out the links for the local businesses that match their respective areas. However, here is an important caveat: *Do not simply copy and paste content while replacing the city names.* This is known as "content spinning," and it stopped working as an effective SEO strategy years ago.

Each page must be unique. A page can express the same thoughts and advice, but the text on the page must not be copied and pasted. Otherwise, you risk your content being labeled as duplicate content by Google, which will hurt its search ranking. Google wants to see unique, high-quality content whenever possible. Yes, this really means writing a unique page for each of the cities you serve. It's a lot of work, but the people who do this inevitably end up capturing far more leads than the people who use a single, one-size-fits-all page targeting the entire area they serve. Those who put in the work will reap the benefits.

To optimize your website for Google's algorithm, you also want to avoid "cannibalizing" your own content. This occurs when you have two web pages optimized and may be ranking for the same keyword. For example, you don't want different pages competing over the term "Santa Clarita IT"—the two pages will cannibalize each other, confuse Google, and, in most cases, impede your rankings. Instead, incorporate as much content about this subject on one page. By consolidating a subject onto a single page, the page will be more authoritative for that keyword and provide additional information to satisfy the intent of that search query. This is why it's crucial to have a preplanned content strategy and trained copywriters to avoid these problems.

A word about co-working spaces and virtual offices: if you don't have a physical presence in a city, it may be tempting to pay a few hundred dollars per month to establish an address in a shared space, just to "be" in the city you're trying to target. Unfortunately, Google generally disregards shared addresses in instances where you can't prove you have your own dedicated space permanently staffed by your own people. (And Google will make you jump through many hoops to prove that your office is real.) This ends up being a waste of time for many businesses. If you don't have a physical presence in a target city, I recommend using the content strategy outlined earlier rather than wasting money on a virtual space that Google will ignore and may even penalize.

CONTENT'S CUMULATIVE EFFECT

As you're creating these similar-but-unique pages for each geographic area in your market, a cumulative effect begins to take place. Every time you publish a page of content, Google crawls your website and indexes the new page. It triggers Google's algorithm to understand that your website is active and becoming more authoritative in a specific niche. It may even reward you with Google's freshness algorithm. The Google freshness update became part of the algorithm in 2011 and is based on Google's belief that content plays a bigger role in answering queries about current news topics than it does about dictionary definitions.

As you publish more content, each page and every individual word on the page populates in the form of a word cloud algorithmically. Then Google semantically associates the words and phrases together while putting more emphasis and authority on the frequency and importance of the topics that you write about most. That is how the algorithm semantically associates you as a thought leader or trusted source with those who are seeking someone with your professional experience. For example, if you are a photographer, you'd want to include content that includes technical terms like aperture, depth of field, and exposure to establish you as a subject expert in your field.

As you publish content that establishes you as a subject expert, your website's relevancy and authority grow. I recommend internally linking related web pages to one another to associate and strengthen the web of content you're creating. For example, suppose you have a page that is optimized for the keyword phrase "Plastic Surgeon in Los Angeles." In such a case, you will need to create a side navigation on the right or left side of the page that links out to all of the other Plastic Surgery pages optimized for other cities, such as Santa Monica and Pasadena, using exact-match anchor text for each respective page.

Even though the links all exist on the same domain—referred to as "internal links"—they still add *tremendous* value. If done correctly, it can be the difference between pushing these pages from page two of Google to the top three positions on page one.

Internal links are one of the most underrated SEO techniques that you can use to dominate your competition with Google.

Remember, Google's definition of popularity largely comes from the quantity and quality of links that are pointing to a given web page. The greatest benefit of internal links is that they're entirely within your control. You have the power to audit your content, find relevant pages, and semantically associate them by way of using internal links and keyword-rich anchor text. Your content builds on itself, cumulatively reinforcing the popularity and authority of each of your pages while passing PageRank and link equity.

THE SKYSCRAPER TECHNIQUE

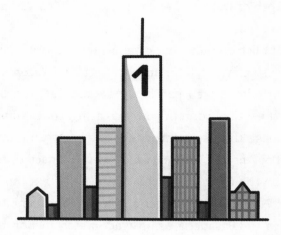

When you Google a search term relevant to your business—"online personal training certification," for example—look at the top results. How can you create a web page better than the competition? What will make your web page outrank the current leaders?

The answer, and a key tool in your content-strategy arsenal, is the Skyscraper Technique. The Skyscraper Technique, coined by Brian Dean, the founder of Backlinko, alludes to the following scenario: You're walking through New York City, admiring the tall buildings that surround you. But have you ever walked by a *really* tall building and said, "Wow, that's amazing. I wonder how big the eighth-tallest building in the world is."? Of course not. It's human nature to be attracted to the best.

What you're doing with this technique is finding the tallest skyscraper in your market in the form of a top-ranking web page on Google and creating one even taller. In that way, you'll have content that Google finds authoritative and that everyone wants to talk about and link to.

Let's say the top-ranking page for "online personal training certification" has 3,000 words of content. To follow the Skyscraper Technique, you might opt to create a page with 5,000 words of content. The goal is to make something better and more comprehensive than what already exists. The Skyscraper strategy involves three easy steps:

- Find a keyword you want to rank for on the first page of Google.
- Analyze what content currently ranks in the top 10 positions on Google.
- Create content that's 10 times better than what is already on the first page.

Once you've created your Skyscraper page, the next step is to reach out to websites linking to the competitor's page and ask them to link to your page instead. Convince them that your content is better—the taller, shinier skyscraper.

YOUR STEP-BY-STEP CONTENT STRATEGY

When we put all of the above advice together, what does this look like? Here is a high-level, step-by-step walk-through of the content strategy process, some of which pulls from the work you did in previous chapters:

- Identify your target audience.
- Identify the markets you currently serve or want to serve.
- Create a list of pillar pages and subtopics generated from keyword research tools and Google's "People Also Ask" (related questions). Also, reverse engineer your competitors' websites for new content ideas.
- Make a spreadsheet containing all the practice areas and geographic locations you want to target. For example, if you're a personal trainer, you might want to create pages about nutrition, weight loss, bodybuilding, and strength training. Plan to create a page for each of the areas in the markets you serve: Santa Clarita, Malibu, Burbank, and Los Angeles. In this example, you would need to write 16 unique pages (four practice

areas for each of the four locations). From there, in the spreadsheet, create the URL structure, title tags, meta descriptions, and header tags that these page templates will follow. Also, give some consideration to how these pages will interlink and pass PageRank.

- Leverage internal links to grow your website's authority and popularity and increase your search rankings.
- Apply the Skyscraper Technique to make your page more authoritative and attract more inbound links, which will also increase your rankings, traffic, leads, and sales.

DON'T OVERCOMPLICATE CONTENT

A huge amount of legwork goes into planning and creating high-quality web pages required to raise your authority with Google, but there's no need to overcomplicate the content process.

At the end of the day, your goal is threefold: become a subject-matter expert, have a presence in your target markets, and create better content than your competitors.

These are simple goals, but don't underinvest in content, either. Remember, Google *is* content, and the content on your website will make or break your search ranking. It's not enough to hire a content writer to publish blog posts without direction or focus—you need a targeted strategy that will position your website above your competitors.

START WITH YOUR BUSINESS'S CORE AREA OF FOCUS

You have dozens, hundreds, or even thousands of web pages to create. Understandably, this can feel overwhelming. You can't create all of your content simultaneously, so where do you start?

I recommend beginning with the practice areas that are most profitable for your business. For example, again, if you're a Santa Clarita–based personal trainer who primarily serves clients who want to start strength training, first write and publish a page optimized for Santa Clarita strength training. From there, continue to build out all of the other sub-practice areas for your Santa Clarita location.

Continue to expand your site, one page at a time, while developing the most trusted and authoritative resource for someone who may be doing research and in need of what you offer. The proven strategy outlined above will provide both the user and Google with what they are looking for while strengthening your site with amazing content, all interlinking to each other like Wikipedia does. This should exponentially compound your traffic, leads, and revenue, month over month.

There's no defined end to this content-creation process because you can always extend your content branches further and cover more topics. The more content you create, the more opportunities you have to draw targeted traffic and prospects to your website. The key is to start close to home with the bread and butter of your business and then build out from there.

TIPS AND TAKEAWAYS: CONTENT STRATEGY

→ Content refers to everything on your website, including text, photos, videos, infographics, and more.

→ Google's algorithm places a huge amount of value on content. Without content, Google wouldn't exist.

→ To get results and boost your search rankings, you need to approach content creation with a strategy that prioritizes your audience, key areas of focus, and target markets.

→ Create localized pages for every geographic area you serve. These can share a similar template and structure, but their content must be 100 percent unique so they don't trigger any duplicate content filters or penalties.

→ Optimize single pages for specific keywords, phrases, and FAQs to avoid cannibalization problems.

→ Leverage the cumulative effect of content by internally linking relevant pages to one another.

→ Apply the Skyscraper Technique to overthrow the current top-ranking web pages of your competitors.

→ Start building web pages for your business's core areas of focus, and then branch out from there.

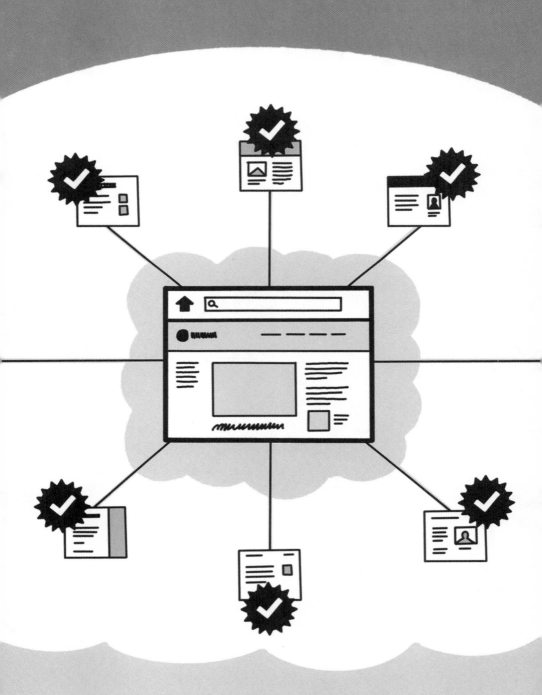

one link at a time.

CHAPTER 8

Increasing Your Website's Popularity One Link at a Time

In Google's vast web, links are the strands that spiders follow from page to page. They bring people to your website, and they can either add to or detract from your credibility. In a way, they're the currency of the web because if you have more high-quality links pointing to your website (called "backlinks") than your competitors have, then your website has more value.

Links play a critical role in your website's ranking in terms of the three SEO components: relevancy, popularity, and integrity. You could have a technically perfect web page with well-crafted, relevant content, but without links adding to its popularity, that web page could still linger in obscurity. Your website needs links and the popularity they bring to secure high rankings within Google's algorithm.

Seek out relevant links

When seeking opportunities for link building, you don't want any old website linking back to yours—you want *relevant* links. Google is sophisticated enough to tell the context and subject of a website by analyzing its keywords, links, and even images, and it assigns more value to links that connect relevant web pages.

If a law school has a link on their website pointing to your law firm's website, the algorithm will consider it much more valuable than, say, a link from a bicycle shop pointing to your website. When relevant and reputable websites link to your website, some of the linking website's PageRank "flows over" and increases your own.

The same applies to relevant pages, even if the linking website as a whole isn't relevant. For example, suppose a news site publishes a story about a bodybuilding competition and links to your personal training website. In that case, Google understands that it's a relevant connection and rewards your site by boosting its popularity.

UNDERSTANDING YOUR LINKS

Links can help or hurt your website's search ranking depending on many factors: where the links come from, whether the links are reciprocal or one way, how many links come from a single domain, the anchor text of the link, and more. Let's break down a few of the main things you should understand about links so you can leverage link-building to increase your Google rankings, lift traffic, and get more customers.

Referring domains

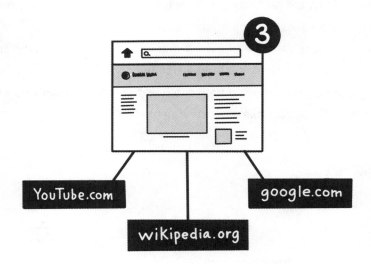

Many of the tools discussed in previous chapters will give you statistics on links, including the total number of backlinks pointing to your website, but in my experience, that's not the most important metric to consider. The more telling indicator of your link strength isn't the number of *links* but rather the number of *referring domains* linking back to your website. Referring domains are websites that link to the target page. Examples include **wikipedia.com**, **youtube.com**, and **google.com**. When analyzing your backlinks, if these three sites were linking to you, they would register as three unique referring domains.

Why is the number of referring domains more important than total backlinks?

Let's say one of your business colleagues has a personal website with 500 pages indexed on Google. They put a link to your company's website in the footer of their website, and all of a sudden, when analyzing your link profile, you see the total number of backlinks pointing to your website jump by 500. You think, *That's great for my site's popularity!* But really, those links are coming from only one referring domain. Don't get me wrong—these links may have value, but not as much as separate referring domains.

It's far more valuable to gain 500 links originating from different referring domains than 500 links from one domain. In fact, having so many links from a single domain can negatively impact your popularity score if Google thinks you're trying to manipulate the system.

Anchor text

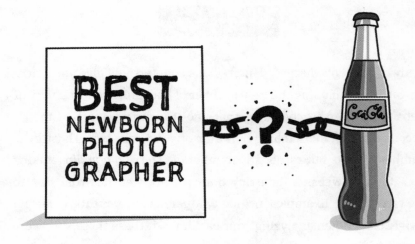

Anchor text is the word or words attached to a link. Usually, anchor text appears underlined and in blue font. Google analyzes the anchor text of a link and surrounding text when determining relevancy, so it's important to think carefully about the words or phrases you choose when adding hyperlinks (anchor text) within the body of your content.

For example, if a blog post contains a link with the anchor text "best newborn photographer," Google connects the relevancy of those keywords used in the anchor text of the link and semantically associates it with the page that you're linking to. That anchor text provides context, whereas if the anchor text attached to the link read "click here," Google wouldn't gain any useful information, and you'd miss out on increasing the SEO of your website.

Google uses all this relevancy and context data surrounding links to combat spam. In the past, people would build links anywhere they could—often in the comment sections of blogs—as a tactic to increase rankings. They would build a link using anchor text like "best newborn photographer" pointing back to their website on a Coca-Cola blog post or forum as a way to leverage Coca-Cola's popularity and authority. Today, Google recognizes that a baby photographer has no relevance to a soft drink company and may discount the value of that link algorithmically or even penalize the offending website.

Protecting your website from link attacks

One threat to be aware of, which I discuss in greater detail in chapter 14, is an attack made by associating your site with toxic links. Competitors might actively attempt to sabotage your SEO efforts by building backlinks to your website on low-quality or spammy websites. For example, if a competitor posts a link to your website on a site that has malware or spreads viruses to users' computers, being associated with that site will hurt your overall SEO. In the same way that high PageRank can help increase your Google rankings, being associated with sites with low PageRank could negatively affect you.

To protect yourself from these attacks, you'll want to have someone monitoring your website for unusual link activity as part of your ongoing SEO efforts. The person monitoring your links should examine all of your backlinks and ask, "Does this link seem out of place? Could it be misconstrued as spam?"

Remember, the website linking out as well as the anchor text should both be relevant to your area of focus. Otherwise, the link's presence may look unnatural. With someone acting as your website's bodyguard, you'll be ready to fill out a disavow file—a way to tell Google "I don't approve of this link"—which will disassociate the offending link from your website. You can determine the authority and respectability of a website by checking its Domain Rating (DR) with a third-party analysis tool like Ahrefs.

AVOIDING GOOGLE JAIL

If your website has been hacked, or worse, the SEO team you've hired has been engaging in black hat SEO practices or stealing content from other websites, you might end up in "Google jail" with what is called a "manual penalty." A manual penalty happens when Google's machine learning identifies a piece of content, link, or program on your website as spam. For example, maybe you forgot to update your WordPress plugins, and now there's a vulnerability on your website that steals visitors' passwords.

When this happens, Google may register a manual penalty that tanks your search ranking and diminishes your traffic overnight. They will also flag all of your indexed content in the SERPs as suspicious with a message that reads, "This site may be hacked." They do this for the protection of users conducting searches to avoid spreading any viruses or malware.

Fortunately, there's a way to undo the damage through Google Search Console.

Google Search Console is the only tool that allows you to have a two-way conversation with Google, so it's your only path for recourse. In Search Console, Google will bring the problem to your attention. Then it's up to you to fix the problem and remove any vulnerabilities. That could be as simple as updating your plugins and removing malware, or as complicated as having to analyze thousands of links pointing back to your website as a victim of a negative SEO attack and creating a complex disavow file to submit to Google.

Once you've fixed the problem, you'll also need to submit what is called a reconsideration request. It could take a few hours to several days for Google to review your request and either remove the penalty or leave it in place. Until someone reviews your case and removes the penalty, your website is stuck in Google jail. It is also worth noting that Google is vague in the way that they communicate these penalties. If you find yourself in this predicament, I highly recommend that you engage an SEO expert who has experience dealing with Google penalties.

LINK BUILDING TAKES REAL WORK

According to Google, if your company is a legitimate business, your website should gain links naturally. It will, but the attitude that your site can rank high with only passive link building isn't realistic. In order to be competitive, you must proactively pursue high-quality links. Where can you build these authoritative links that will help increase your rankings?

Here are a few ideas to gain high-quality backlinks:

> **Niche directories.** It might cost you a few hundred dollars for a listing in a reputable niche directory, but the link pointing back to your website may be worth every penny. To find these, just do a Google search with your business's niche in mind. If you do plastic surgery, for example, just type that in, plus keywords like "association," "directories," "Masterminds," or "groups to associate."
>
> **Better Business Bureau.** The BBB is a trusted and highly respected website with a Domain Rating of 93 at the time of writing this book, which makes it one of the most valuable backlinks any business could have.
>
> **Social media.** Your YouTube page and other social media profiles should each provide a link to your website. With Domain Ratings usually in the high 90s (meaning Google recognizes the website's importance), links from these social channels can pass both PageRank and TrustRank, depending on the attribute of the link. Be aware that while you don't want to duplicate content on your own website, it's fine to have the same videos on your YouTube and Vimeo channels and other comparable platforms.

Scholarships. You can get backlinks from universities and other academic websites by sponsoring a student scholarship.

Interviews. Have someone from an industry news website or blog interview you. The resulting article should contain a link pointing to your website.

Podcasts. Whether you host your own podcast or are a guest, this is a great way to get more exposure and build authoritative links.

Government and higher education. If you can establish your website as a reliable information source or form a partnership with a government agency or university, you might be able to secure a backlink from a .gov or .edu site. Google knows that not just anyone can publish on a government or higher education website, and therefore, these sources make for exceptionally strong links.

Press releases. Put out a press release on topics like your involvement with charity, the announcement of a new service, relocating your office, and more. If the release gets picked up by a media outlet, it will link to your website. Since most news sites curate old content, I would encourage you to write and syndicate a press release at least every three months.

Job websites. Post open job opportunities to websites like LinkedIn, Indeed, ZipRecruiter, Career Builder, Glassdoor, and Monster, and include a link to your website from either your company profile or the individual job description.

Review websites. Make sure your business has a

presence on websites like Yelp and encourage your customers or clients to post reviews.

Business directories. Listing your business on websites like **yellowpages.com**, **botw.org**, **chamberofcommerce. com**, and **superpages.com** are easy, quick link-building wins.

Community media. Another effective strategy for gaining backlinks is community involvement. Whether you sponsor a local little league team or engage in some other kind of giving, your website can get backlinked on community web pages, local news sites, social media, and more.

Competitors. For more ideas on building backlinks, run your competitors' websites through a link-analysis tool like Ahrefs, Semrush, or Majestic. See which websites point to them and try to gain the same links.

Not only will these backlinks directly result in more traffic from people clicking on them, but they'll indirectly boost traffic by increasing your website's popularity with higher search rankings.

Publishing on external blogs

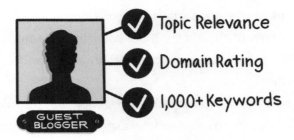

As a subject-matter expert, it can be a win-win scenario for you to publish articles on other people's websites or blogs. This technique is called guest blogging. The site owner gets content, which will increase their traffic, and you get exposure and a backlink, which will increase your rankings and traffic.

However, before you can start publishing, you need to find relevant and authoritative sites that will accept and publish your articles. This requires manual outreach and relationship building. Don't be surprised if the owner of a site asks for a monetary administrative fee for their time to review and publish your article. In fact, some site owners might even offer to write an article either for or about you, saving you the time and money in content creation. Just make sure that you can review and approve the content before it gets published. In this case, this would be no different than paying a writer to write an article for you.

Now, you might have read that paying for a link goes against Google's quality guidelines, and while this "administrative fee" may be loosely interpreted as an exchange of money for a link, if it's executed correctly, the reward is much greater than the risk.

After practicing SEO for over two decades, I can say with great certainty that in order to rank high on Google for competitive key-words, this technique is very effective. Don't get me wrong, this strategy is not easy and requires a lot of manual labor. However, the more effort you put in to identify and establish relationships with relevant blog owners that meet your minimum requirements, which we talk about shortly, the more your total number of referring domains will grow, leading to increased rankings, traffic, leads, and customer sales.

If you work with a digital marketing agency, they probably already have relationships with bloggers who may accept your content. These bloggers might consider you a subject-matter expert and ask you to contribute one-off articles or even offer you your own feature column.

What metrics should you look at when analyzing guest blog opportunities? The metrics we use at Hennessey Digital include the following:

- Sites that are relevant to a specific niche
- Sites with a Domain Rating (DR) of 30 or greater using Ahrefs
- Sites that rank on Google for at least 1,000 keywords based on Semrush's organic keyword trends

The best way to judge whether a guest blog opportunity is worth an administrative fee is by making sure the site in question meets these minimum metrics. Look at the site design and the historical content published, and take into account your overall gut feeling based on your communication and interactions with the owner of the site. If the site has a high Domain Rating, meaning it's popular and authoritative, is topically related, and meets all of the other requirements, the opportunity may justify the cost.

Some webmasters might be happy to post your content in exchange for the future traffic they will receive, while others may ask for an administrative fee ranging anywhere from $15 to $500. Don't settle for their first price. I've seen administrative fees get reduced substantially just by negotiating.

Another approach is to reverse engineer your competitors' link profiles. You can even begin to reverse engineer strategies from businesses in bigger markets than yours. For instance, if you are a massage therapist in a small market, conduct a Google search for a massage therapist in Los Angeles, Orlando, or New York. Now, take the URL of their home page and put it into Ahrefs, the link analysis tool we've already discussed. From there, click on referring domains and sort their links by Domain Rating, highest to lowest. Finally, download all of the links onto a spreadsheet and compare them to all of the links you have pointing back to your website. Suppose the highest-ranking massage therapy spas in the country have links from a particular site. In that case, it's a strong signal that Google is using these links when calculating the authority of their site.

OUT-LINK YOUR COMPETITORS

Always remember that your goal with SEO is not just to match the top players in your market but to surpass them. Set goals for yourself to build a certain number of backlinks per month and look for ways to gain a competitive advantage. Because Google search results are so localized, you're not competing with the entire world, only with the top companies in your specific market. Constantly ask yourself and your digital marketing team, "What will help our web pages rank higher than theirs?"

If the top-ranking companies in your area have a link from a particular directory, you should have the same. You'll need to have as many or more high-quality backlinks to surpass the competition.

Whether it's writing content, recording videos, talking to interviewers, podcasting, submitting press releases, getting involved in the community, or simply submitting to be in directories, each of these activities takes time and effort to do right. You'll need someone writing content, someone doing email outreach, someone researching places to build links, someone handling social media, and more. Link building, like SEO as a whole, is a team effort.

As you can see, link building is not as simple as "the more links, the better." You must be scrupulous about which websites are associated with your own. Inbound links and the anchor text used within the link should be relevant and from a trusted and authoritative source. Take a slow and steady approach to link building, and over time, you'll see real growth in your website's traffic while increasing your leads and customer sales.

WHAT LINKS CONTRIBUTE TO ACHIEVING TOP RANK ON GOOGLE?

Over the past two decades, I have reverse engineered the link strategies being used to top-rank on Google for some of the most competitive and expensive legal keywords on the internet. These keywords include "mesothelioma lawyer," "cerebral palsy lawyer," "New York personal injury lawyer," and dozens of others.

My team and I have invested hundreds of hours researching, analyzing, and studying the link patterns from over 5,000 law firms, looking to see what the top-ranking websites all have in common in terms of their link profiles. Based on this data, I can confidently say that if you can get links from the following domains, although not an easy task, you will take your SEO to the next level and start to dominate your market.

These websites are ranked by their Domain Rating, as specified by the SEO tool Ahrefs at the time of this writing. The higher the number, the more a link from that website can help your own site.

Top fifty foundational links

Foundational Link (Domain Rating)

facebook.com (100)

youtube.com (98)

linkedin.com (98)

pinterest.com (97)

en.wikipedia.org (95)

vimeo.com (95)

reddit.com (94)

creativecommons.org (94)

blogger.com (94)

yelp.com (94)

flickr.com (94)

bbb.org (93)

bing.com (93)

behance.net (93)

eventbrite.com (93)

medium.com (93)

sites.google.com (93)

yahoo.com (92)

business.site (91)

mapquest.com (91)

meetup.com (91)

prnewswire.com (91)

wikihow.com (91)

businesswire.com (91)

about.me (90)

glassdoor.com (90)

indeed.com (90)

provenexpert.com (90)

prweb.com (90)

yellowpages.com (90)

crunchbase.com (89)

expertise.com (86)

scoop.it (86)

superpages.com (85)

visual.ly (85)

citysearch.com (84)

diigo.com (84)

prlog.org (84)

newswire.com (81)

chamberofcommerce.com (80)

company.com (80)

theodysseyonline.com (80)

topratedlocal.com (80)

dandb.com (79)

local.com (79)

muckrack.com (79)

dexknows.com (78)

ezlocal.com (78)

folkd.com (78)

botw.org (74)

Top 100 news and media links

News and Media Link (Domain Rating)

news.microsoft.com (96)

forbes.com (93)

nytimes.com (93)

theguardian.com (93)

cnn.com (93)

bbc.com (92)

bloomberg.com (92)

businessinsider.com (92)

usatoday.com (92)

washingtonpost.com (92)

wsj.com (92)

abcnews.go.com (92)

npr.org (92)

cnbc.com (92)

reuters.com (92)

wired.com (92)

hbr.org (92)

fortune.com (92)

time.com (92)

huffpost.com (91)

cbsnews.com (91)

bizjournals.com (91)

buzzfeed.com (91)

dailymotion.com (91)

entrepreneur.com (91)

fastcompany.com (91)

inc.com (91)

latimes.com (91)

marketwatch.com (91)

msn.com (91)

nbcnews.com (91)

theatlantic.com (91)

mashable.com (91)

usnews.com (91)

vice.com (91)

newyorker.com (91)

ft.com (91)

apnews.com (90)

bostonglobe.com (90)

cbslocal.com (90)

chicagotribune.com (90)

chron.com (90)

foxnews.com (90)

news.yahoo.com (90)

newsweek.com (90)

nymag.com (90)

nypost.com (90)

nydailynews.com (90)

people.com (90)

sfgate.com (90)

theconversation.com (90)

today.com (90)

vox.com (90)

patch.com (90)

rollingstone.com (90)

vogue.com (90)

boston.com (89)

seattletimes.com (89)

buzzfeednews.com (89)

vanityfair.com (89)

startribune.com (89)

cosmopolitan.com (89)

foxbusiness.com (89)

ap.org (88)

mercurynews.com (88)

nj.com (88)

msnbc.com (87)

dallasnews.com (87)

ajc.com (87)

denverpost.com (87)

ibtimes.com (87)

salon.com (87)

oregonlive.com (87)

sfchronicle.com (87)

baltimoresun.com (87)

insider.com (87)

esquire.com (87)

gq.com (87)

newsday.com (86)

cleveland.com (86)

rd.com (86)

sandiegouniontribune.com (86)

menshealth.com (86)

womenshealthmag.com (86)

mlive.com (85)

al.com (85)

detroitnews.com (85)

houstonchronicle.com (85)

ocregister.com (85)

orlandosentinel.com (85)

sacbee.com (85)

sun-sentinel.com (85)

washingtonexaminer.com (85)

money.com (84)

mic.com (84)

newrepublic.com (84)

reviewjournal.com (84)

laweekly.com (84)

natlawreview.com (83)

bloomberglaw.com (83)

Top 100 educational (.edu) links

Educational (.edu) Link (Domain Rating)

harvard.edu (92)

stanford.edu (92)

berkeley.edu (91)

princeton.edu (91)

cmu.edu (91)

columbia.edu (91)

psu.edu (91)

cornell.edu (91)

ucla.edu (91)

umich.edu (91)

twin-cities.umn.edu (91)

upenn.edu (91)

washington.edu (91)

wisc.edu (91)

yale.edu (91)

duke.edu (90)

illinois.edu (90)

msu.edu (90)

nyu.edu (90)

purdue.edu (90)

ucdavis.edu (90)

uchicago.edu (90)

uci.edu (90)

ufl.edu (90)

ucsd.edu (90)

usc.edu (90)

utexas.edu (90)

osu.edu (90)

northwestern.edu (90)

rutgers.edu (90)

unc.edu (90)

tamu.edu (90)

arizona.edu (89)

ncsu.edu (89)

virginia.edu (89)

bu.edu (89)

indiana.edu (89)

gatech.edu (88)

georgetown.edu (88)

iu.edu (88)

oregonstate.edu (88)

tufts.edu (88)

ucsf.edu (88)

colostate.edu (88)

cuny.edu (88)

hawaii.edu (88)

pitt.edu (88)

ucsb.edu (88)

unl.edu (88)

byu.edu (87)

caltech.edu (87)

rochester.edu (87)

uga.edu (87)

uiowa.edu (87)

umass.edu (87)

vanderbilt.edu (87)

gwu.edu (87)

wsu.edu (87)

dartmouth.edu (86)

ucsc.edu (86)

fsu.edu (86)

gmu.edu (86)

missouri.edu (86)

nd.edu (86)

uky.edu (86)

uoregon.edu (86)

usf.edu (86)

emory.edu (86)

ku.edu (86)

rice.edu (86)

uic.edu (86)

buffalo.edu (85)

miami.edu (85)

uconn.edu (85)

unm.edu (85)

northeastern.edu (85)

rit.edu (85)

temple.edu (85)

bc.edu (85)

utk.edu (85)

lsu.edu (84)

ucr.edu (84)

uh.edu (84)

case.edu (84)

drexel.edu (84)

fiu.edu (84)

sc.edu (84)

vcu.edu (84)

american.edu (83)

auburn.edu (83)

smu.edu (83)

umaryland.edu (83)

wvu.edu (83)

jhsph.edu (83)

ua.edu (83)

uab.edu (83)

baylor.edu (82)

calpoly.edu (81)

bucknell.edu (78)

syracuse.edu (78)

Top four data aggregators

Data Aggregator (Domain Rating)

foursquare.com (92)

factual.com (75)

local-listings.data-axle.com (77)

neustarlocaleze.biz (73)

You can submit your website to all four of these data aggregators with any of the following paid services:

yext.com

brightlocal.com

moz.com

synup.com

advicelocal.com

→ Links contribute to your website's popularity and can either add to or detract from your credibility.

→ To increase your popularity, you need relevant links pointing to your website. Irrelevant websites linking to yours may look suspicious to Google and might create problems.

→ When analyzing your link-building activity, it's more important to look at how many referring domains point to your site than how many links you have total. You could have thousands of links coming from a single domain, and not only would it do little to boost your popularity, but it might actually lower it. A diverse selection of referring domains conveys more authority.

→ Google analyzes the text surrounding a link as well as the link text itself, called "anchor text," to determine a link's context and relevancy.

→ Competitors can maliciously attack your website by using negative SEO link strategies. Combat this by constantly monitoring your backlink profile and then submit a disavow file when necessary to disassociate your website with these potentially toxic links.

→ If Google suspects you of breaking its rules, your website might get a manual penalty. You'll then need to use Google

continued

Search Console to fix any problems and submit a reconsideration request.

→ Link building takes a huge amount of ongoing work and consistent effort. There's no end to the number of valuable links you can build through directories, social media, blogging, press releases, and more.

→ To successfully outrank your competitors in search results, you must have at least as many trusted and authoritative links as they do.

BECOME Remarkable

CHAPTER 9

PR and Marketing

You might've noticed that a lot of what we talked about—from garnering press to securing a guest post—technically qualifies as marketing. And you'd be right. Marketing and PR is an umbrella term that stands for the host of activities that can generate attention to your business, increase brand awareness, and convert real leads.

Marketing and PR are essential to any business, as they drive growth, leads, and sales. A business that spends time only on building a product and not marketing it cannot survive in the long term.

One way to think about SEO is as the best, most reliable marketing channel there is, with Google having the largest amount of leads in the world. But in this chapter, for the purposes of SEO, we focus on PR and marketing as it relates directly to link building, and what that usually means is securing press coverage, securing a spot on a podcast, and more. I teach you how to do this, and in the process, teach you the fundamentals of PR and marketing that'll be the foundation for all of your marketing efforts going forward.

BECOMING REMARKABLE

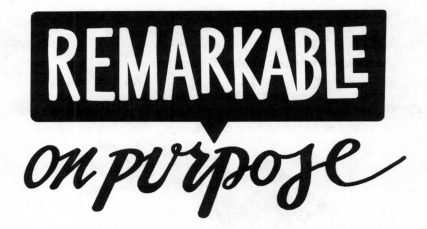

It might feel that getting attention—a scarce commodity that is so precious these days—can be challenging. And I understand. Particularly in the beginning, getting and maintaining attention to your business, your cause, or your product can be tough, especially in a world where there are so many things clamoring for people's attention.

But attention is the critical ingredient to having a successful business, whether you choose to engage in SEO or not. If there is no attention to your business, there will be no one to buy your product or your services.

What this means is that getting attention (from the right people and in the right way) *is* marketing, and the best way to set up the foundation for this is to *become remarkable*.

In Seth Godin's book *Purple Cow*, he writes about how you probably wouldn't tell anyone if you saw a pasture filled with brown cows. But if you saw a *purple* cow, you'd talk to people about it. The key is in the word *remarkable*—it's the quality of something people want to *remark* about.

For all your PR and marketing efforts going forward, remember that you have to become remarkable. It's a quality everyone can reverse engineer in themselves and their businesses.

BELIEVE YOU ARE REMARKABLE

A lot of people do not believe they're remarkable. They may believe that their businesses are boring. Maybe you sell napkins or affordable jeans. Maybe you feel that your life, on the whole, is a little routine and boring. If you have this mindset, you might not get far with your marketing efforts.

There's a bit of a self-fulfilling prophecy effect going on here: if you believe you're remarkable, you can start to become remarkable.

In the same way that you can feel the confidence or lack of it in someone who speaks to you, people can *feel* when you believe that you're worthy of receiving attention and praise. Your lack of self-belief will filter into your marketing. If you do not believe you're interesting, you'll create uninteresting marketing campaigns, pitches, and stories. Reporters won't want to pick them up. If you feel you have an uninteresting business, it'll come across in the pitch, people will feel it, and you won't get media coverage or get booked on podcasts.

Of course, you don't have to be arrogant or out of touch with reality—don't believe things that are untrue. But if you start with the mindset that you have the potential to be remarkable, then you'll be much more successful in your PR efforts.

DIFFERENTIATE YOURSELF FROM YOUR COMPETITORS

Once you believe on some level that you're remarkable (or that you have the potential to become remarkable), it's time to understand how to differentiate yourself from your competitors.

Whatever niche you're in, your competitors will have a very specific style, language, and way of interacting with the world. Since people tend to copy other people (it's human nature), a lot of your competitors will do similar things.

Now, some of these things that people copy are for good reasons. But most of it is simply because we're human, and we like to conform to what other people are doing. So I'd like to encourage you to go in the opposite direction, if only a little bit.

What are you doing that is different from your competitors? What about your current marketing and personality—how is that different from the companies you compete with? And how can you take what you're already doing (even if it's just selling napkins) and turn it into something interesting?

A lot of people forget that people like Gary Vaynerchuk, one of the most influential thought leaders in the world, started out without the glitz and glamor. In the beginning, these influential people were just like you, doing things to get the ball rolling and to drive attention. Gary Vaynerchuk was selling wine, but he made it interesting with Wine Library TV, where he created engaging videos on YouTube that benefited from the force of his brazen personality.

Another example is TOMS. At first glance, TOMS is just another shoe company. But they did something interesting and remarkable. Rather than simply selling shoes, they decided to try a different model—for every shoe they sold, they gave away a pair to youths in Argentina or other developing countries. This generated press, and if you know TOMS, it's probably because of this very story. They created a fundamentally new business model and the media was excited to talk about what they were doing.

What can you do that's different—in style, in design, in the way you do things, in the way you market something? Is it in your personality or your view of the world? Are you bold in an industry that's meek? Is your product different in a way that catches people's attention—or is it something else that sets you apart?

Find the difference between you and your competitors and you will find what makes you remarkable. Grab a notebook and map out what makes you different, listing out each quality. Write down what you could do in the future that would heighten the difference between you and your competitors.

DO REMARKABLE THINGS

Remarkable people do remarkable things. Even if you don't think you are remarkable to begin with, the best way to become remarkable is to do things that will get people talking.

You can even think of marketing as the art of doing things that *are* remarkable. The more remarkable things you do, the more people will talk about your company, your brand, and who you are—and the more likely that'll translate to more links, more leads, more sales, and more clients.

You can do remarkable things in two ways: finding the things you're doing that are already remarkable, and intentionally setting out to do new remarkable things. Both are important from a strategic point of view. Building remarkability into a news story or a guest blog post or leveraging remarkability you already have will go a long way toward increasing the effectiveness of your marketing efforts.

I grew up in relative poverty, and my mother experienced severe medical issues when I was a child. Life was financially and emotionally difficult. But the difficulty of those early years was pivotal in fostering the sense of motivation I have now. My own hardships and the result of growing from those experiences became the basis for press pieces I was able to land (in places like *Forbes*, *Yahoo! Finance*, etc.) because it was an interesting story hook and it was something that was intrinsically remarkable.

Another example is that I took improv comedy after my time in the air force. I'd always loved comedy, but what surprised me was that the same qualities that helped me in improv also helped me become a business leader. When I had someone who worked for me point this out, this became the basis for an article that I published on *Inc.* titled "Why Every Entrepreneur Should Take an Improv Class." It fit the publication and the style they were looking for, but most importantly, it was remarkable because it was decidedly unconventional.

What stands out about these examples is that they were things that I'd *already* done, and we turned them into news stories. One exercise you can do right now is try to pick out (preferably with a partner) things in your life that are *already* remarkable and might make for a compelling core to a press piece you could pitch. Keep writing down ideas until you hit on a few that show promise.

Everyone has these stories in one form or another. It's just a matter of remembering them and bringing them back to the surface. Being transparent with yourself and your business helps. Many people, understandably, want to hide behind a facade. But if you're able to be transparent and reveal things about your life that are remarkable, you can gain a competitive edge. As I like to say: make your mess your message. Don't be afraid to be vulnerable.

And if you feel like you need to be more intentional about your remarkability, brainstorming is your friend. Generate ideas that you can put into action. When you're evaluating ideas, evaluate whether the idea fits in with your brand. And ask yourself these questions: Is this different? Is this interesting? Is this worth other people talking about?

Once you have an idea, all you have to do is go out and make it happen.

MANAGING PR

Once you have your mindset right, you'll be ready to get started.

Managing PR can be simplified into these four steps:

1. **Craft your story.** Line up your story idea, which will be a remarkable one, of course!
2. **Compile your media list.** This should consist of authoritative journalists, writers, podcasters, and bloggers to whom you will pitch your story idea.
3. **Pitch your story angle to the media.** If they say yes, you'll work with the journalist to help craft and provide details for them to write an interesting article.
4. **Leverage the result by sharing it on social media.** This should create new media opportunities.

For the purposes of this book, I highlight the basic and most effective points that'll help you land press, with the intention of growing your business and, more critically, bolstering SEO.

Let's get started.

Step #1: Crafting your story

If you've already completed the brainstorming exercises in the previous section, you've already started crafting your story. By now, being remarkable is a mindset, and you're ready to use it to your advantage.

The next steps are pretty simple. Out of all the brainstorming sections you've compiled, pick a story you'd like to use. Write down your story in under half a page.

A skilled writer or PR person can help you with this, but your story needs to have a couple of qualities. First, you want a story that's remarkable. Try testing it out with friends: How do they react when you tell them the story? Underwhelmed? Intrigued?

The second quality is that the story should look attractive to a journalist and make sense within a news program or a blog (depending on the type of outlet you're trying to land press for—more on this in the next section). This is more of an instinct, but an attractive story should fit into the type of topics, formats, and ideas that journalists and bloggers like to cover.

Keep in mind that the internet is a huge place. A good story for a mom blog is not the same as a good story for *Forbes*, so understand that a good story in one context may be a bad story in another. Instead, try to create a story that maps onto your target audience.

You want to land on websites whose domains are directly relevant to yours, so your story should be entertaining, informative, or interesting to the target demographic of your customers. Not only does this help increase your brand awareness, but it also helps Google understand a semantic association when the website links back to you. Remember, relevancy is a core part of your SEO strategy.

Step #2: Compiling a media list

Now that you've crafted a loose version of your story, identify your media list. Who are the journalists, the bloggers, and the reporters most likely to be interested in your story? Where would you go online to learn more about companies with a similar story, service, or product? Write all of this down on a spreadsheet, which will become a tool for your PR outreach efforts.

What's great is that finding journalists online is as easy as looking them up. Most journalists, bloggers, and reporters have their contact information online, and using paid services like MuckRack or Cision, you can find and compile media lists even faster, with names, phone numbers, and emails.

However you look for them, whether it's through Google, finding publications that cover similar topics, or finding articles similar to your own and researching the journalists (all three of which are great strategies), always discern whether or not these people would want to hear from you. Does the media list you're compiling consist of targeted writers who would be interested in hearing a story like yours? Or is it random?

The key to getting media attention is to pitch precisely to your target audience, to pitch frequently (you'll be getting a lot of rejections), and to pitch well. Make sure your media list is composed of people who are intrigued by your story and people who write for your target audience.

Step #3: Pitching and building relationships

The most important thing to understand is that journalists are inundated with pitches. Pitching does work, but in order to land press, it's important to understand a few things.

First, quantity is important to pitching. My executive coach is Cameron Herold, who co-wrote with Adrian Salamunovic the book *Free PR*. He maintains that to land just five pieces of press, plan to pitch 100. That means there will be a lot of rejection involved, and you need to see rejection as part of the process.

So don't be discouraged. As you get more press, it'll come more easily. The best type of press, fortunately, is natural press. Once you start getting more stories placed, you'll get to a point where you become friends with journalists and bloggers, and the press happens more effortlessly.

In the beginning, it'll take a little bit of effort to get going. Take time to plan before you pitch. Craft an attractive angle and understand that every publication is different. I recommend training someone to pitch for you using the book *Free PR* as a training manual.

While the story you're pitching might be the same, tweak your email pitch for each publication and journalist. Try to include things that make it clear it's tailored for them: a compelling subject line that mentions something they'd be interested in, a reference to their work, any friends in common (if possible), as well as adequate social proof that validates you as a person or your unique company story.

Then comes your pitch. You want to hook them in three to five sentences about why your story is remarkable and why it would be great for their audience.

Earlier, I told you to compile phone numbers as well. Since reporters get hundreds of emails a day, it's easy to get lost in the flood. But a phone number can be priceless. If you call reporters with the question, "Hey, I've got a great story for you—do you have two minutes?," most of them will say yes. If you or your PR person is able to explain precisely what the story is and tailor the pitch to intrigue their audience, in my experience for Hennessey Digital, we've had a very high acceptance rate for stories that we've pitched by phone.

Remember to follow up and be persistent but not annoying. Follow up twice, but not too soon—give it a week or so for them to get back to you.

Once you've secured a piece of press coverage, you'll work with the journalist, blogger, or reporter to make the story happen. This might involve being interviewed by the reporter, emailing them back and forth to fill out details, or providing headshots and other visual assets for the story. Whatever is needed, you'll work to make sure the story is secured while building new relationships.

One of the most important things to keep in mind is that the entire point of doing this, from an SEO perspective, is to get a story that links back to your website. Without a backlink, your site won't gain the maximum SEO benefit.

Of course, I wouldn't say there's no SEO value without it—there's still value in co-citations (when a website mentions you without linking to you) or co-occurrences (when a website mentions keywords related to you without linking to you). But links are best, so it's good to focus on them.

Step #4: You've landed the story—now what?

Once you've landed press, take a moment to congratulate yourself. It's a victory for your business. The next step is to simply leverage it. Once you have a story (or four) landed, you can take that story and use it to your advantage, furthering your SEO and getting the most out of the press.

The first step is to share it on social media and watch as your links, rankings, traffic, and leads start to grow. The more people you share it with, the higher the chances the story will spread organically. And since spreading it on social media is as easy as a sentence and a click, you should use it.

The next step is to leverage the story to get more interviews and more press. Getting press is surprisingly powerful social proof that shows journalists you are worthy of press. While having a remarkable angle increases your chances of being covered, effective social proof can seal the deal.

Lastly, get your press framed and hung in your office for clients, prospects, and employees to see. Press can help bolster motivation and trust in you and what you offer—and the more people who see that, the more effective you'll be at doing what you do. For some prospects, the difference between press and no press can be the difference between someone you meet once and someone with whom you build a trusted business relationship that lasts into the future.

PRESS RELEASES

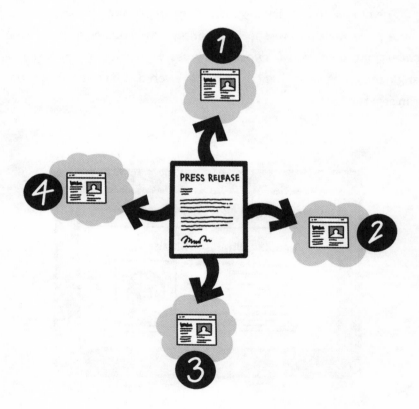

In addition to the prescribed steps to getting press, you should also be leveraging newswire services like PR Newswire, Accesswire, PRWeb, and 24-7 Press Release. These services take your press release and send it out to be published by different news organizations and media outlets. Because each one has different syndication places (though some will have overlap), they will syndicate your press release to different news outlets.

As a good SEO practice, I tend to cycle through newswire services for each press release I put out. For one press release, I might use PR Newswire. For the next, I might use PRWeb. This helps me get different links, which only strengthens my overall SEO.

If you pay for a newswire service to syndicate your press release, there's a 100 percent chance you'll be featured on news sites that syndicate for that specific newswire. Think of it like an automatic blog feed: when you publish a press release with Accesswire, there are numerous news pieces that'll automatically publish your press release word for word. If you link back to your website *in* your press release, that means when they syndicate it, high-ranking news sites will link back to your piece as well, giving you the benefit of a high-ranking news site backlink.

That said, whether or not a journalist will actually see your press release and write an original story is a different matter. It's entirely possible that you put out a press release and no journalists pick it up (other than automatic syndication).

Whether or not they pick it up is dependent on a lot of factors, including timing, the remarkability of your story, and whether or not the right journalists see it and decide to write about it.

However, press releases have a great way of instigating opportunities. When journalists, podcasters, or interested parties see your press release, real things can happen as a result—people reach out, interview opportunities open up, and even investment opportunities appear. So while it's possible that none of these things will happen, a press release is still a great part of a larger SEO strategy.

Post it on your own website

The first step to leveraging this strategy is to first post the press release on your own website. It's important that you do this before actually syndicating your press release, because you'll want media sites to link to *your* site. You'll also want a dedicated section on your website that features all of your press releases in one spot, so when people want to learn about your business, all of your press releases are right there. Plus, when you post the press release on your website, Google indexes the article first.

Once you've posted your press release, syndicate it using one of the newswire services (PR Newswire, Accesswire, PRWeb, 24-7 Press Release). A high-profile news organization linking back to your website as well as your original press release will not only improve your SEO but will also increase the consistency of your press efforts by keeping all of the press you've put out in one place.

→ In order to effectively get press coverage and get others to talk about you, you must adopt a "remarkable" mindset. Remarkability is the quality of someone wanting to remark upon you or your company.

→ To become remarkable, you must believe that you are remarkable, differentiate yourself from your competitors, and, most importantly, do remarkable things. Brainstorm remarkable ideas and then choose one for a potential press story.

→ Getting press is valuable because it lends you the domain authority of the news site (or media outlet) and gives you a powerful backlink that strengthens your SEO.

→ Managing PR consists of crafting your story, compiling a media list of people who would want that story, and ultimately pitching, landing, and leveraging each successful placement while building relationships.

→ After you land press, leverage it by sharing it on social media, using it as social proof to land more press and interviews, and get the article framed to show to future clients, prospects, and even employees.

→ Press releases are a great way to get more press for your story, though it may cost you money to submit for distribution.

continued

→   To successfully distribute a press release, post it first on
    your website, then syndicate it with a newswire service.
    Make sure the media sites that pick it up link back to the
    original press release on your website.

TECHNICAL

S E O

101

CHAPTER 10

Technical SEO

By now, you have a solid understanding of how SEO impacts your website's search ranking. You're prepared to hire a digital marketing team, build a content strategy, and acquire the tools you need to achieve and measure success.

I've covered the basics, which leads us to the next step: the advanced concepts of technical SEO.

Technical SEO encompasses topics like URL structure and crawl errors—things that you don't need to understand in detail but should know enough about to recognize when there's a problem. If these issues carry on unnoticed, your Google rankings may suffer, or it may even prevent your website from getting indexed at all, so you want to quickly correct them when they occur.

My goal with this chapter is to arm you with enough information to hire a technical SEO specialist and hold them accountable. Too often, people expect their web developer, the person who builds the website, to understand technical SEO; but technical SEO requires a completely different skill set. I recommend interviewing the agency you hire and confirming that they have a specialist handling technical SEO audits, not a jack-of-all-trades. You want someone laser-focused on technical SEO; otherwise, technical problems on your website could easily go undiscovered.

Again, to find someone qualified and hold them accountable, there's no need to be a technical expert yourself. But it can help to know the basics. Imagine taking your car to the mechanic for an inspection. You don't need to know how to service the car yourself, but you should be aware that an oil change is part of routine maintenance. It's the same for technical SEO.

You should have your specialist audit your website for technical problems weekly, or monthly at the least. If you work with a reputable SEO agency, they will likely have a technical SEO expert or team of experts who monitor for problems on your website daily.

TECHNICAL SEO PROBLEMS

What problems might show up on the technical side of your website? Among other issues, your technical SEO expert should monitor for these:

- Crawl depth inefficiencies
- Cannibalizing pages
- Duplicated content
- Broken links
- Crawl errors
- Slow PageSpeed
- Mobile accessibility
- URL structure issues

If you feel overwhelmed by the idea of technical problems, I'll break down some of the issues listed above. But remember, you only need to know enough to be aware that these problems might exist and ensure your professionals have them covered.

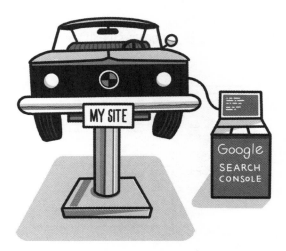

IDENTIFY PROBLEMS USING GOOGLE SEARCH CONSOLE

I mention Google Search Console throughout the book, but I want to remind you of its importance in terms of technical SEO. Like a mechanic plugging a diagnostics tool into a car's onboard system, Google Search Console scans your website and identifies any problems.

It's your best tool for identifying technical issues with your website, whether they're accidental or caused by an attack or hack. The console also empowers you to have a two-way conversation with Google so you can resolve your problems and get your website back in the search engine's good graces. It's like being able to whisper directly into Google's ear, and it doesn't cost a dime to use.

STEP-BY-STEP TECHNICAL AUDIT

To help you understand the role your technical SEO expert will play in your overall digital strategy, let's take a step-by-step look at the questions they'll ask as they audit your website.

Question #1: Is there more than one version of your website?

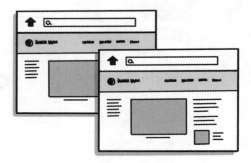

When Google indexes your website, it's important that it only looks at one canonical version. Typically, there are multiple variants that Google *could* be indexing, including but not limited to these:

- **https://www.yourwebsite.com**
- **https://yourwebsite.com**
- **http://www.yourwebsite.com**
- **http://yourwebsite.com**

These are a few of the different ways a user might type your website URL into a browser—either with "www." or without, and either with the secure sockets layer (SSL) "s" in "https" or without.

It's best to choose one of the variants and redirect all others to your chosen canonical version to avoid problems. I would recommend choosing one of the HTTPS secure URLs because security is a top priority for Google, and their goal is to make the internet safer, more broadly. On August 7, 2014, they even confirmed that HTTPS is a ranking signal in their algorithm, albeit small, in a blog post that can be found on Google's Search Central Blog. Whether or not you choose to include "www." is a matter of preference. What's most important is choosing one URL and being consistent with its usage.

Question #2: Are there any crawl errors?

Next, your technical SEO expert will want to crawl your website using a tool that helps you identify, audit, and improve common SEO issues. I recommend one called Screaming Frog SEO Spider, which crawls your website in the same way Google would crawl it.

Screaming Frog SEO Spider will start at your home page and then follow every link located on every page of your website and in the source code. Depending on how big your website is, it could take as little as five minutes or as much as five hours to finish crawling every page and populating the data.

When the tool is finished, it will show you the crawl depth of each page—this is how many links the tool had to follow from the home page to the destination page. Most pages will have a depth of two or three. If you have pages buried as deep as 16 or 17, you'll want to fix your internal linking structure to bring them closer to the home page, also known as the root.

This tool also allows you to analyze internal and external links, HTTP response codes, URL structure, page titles, meta descriptions, header tags, image file sizes, and canonical or pagination issues. Now, if this all sounds foreign to you, that's okay. This is why I recommend finding someone who knows what they're doing with technical SEO.

Question #3: Are any pages ranking for the same keyword?

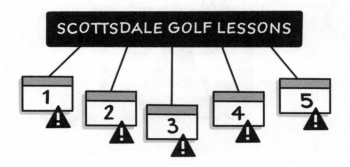

For every keyword or phrase relevant to your business, like "Scottsdale golf lessons" and "Scottsdale golf pro," you'll want to make sure there is only a single page optimized for this keyword and all the semantically related keywords. For example, Google understands that "Scottsdale golf lessons" or "Scottsdale golf pro" mean the same thing. While I would recommend including these different variations within the H2 and H3 tags (the smaller headlines you see halfway down a web page) and in the body copy of the "Scottsdale golf lessons" page, you wouldn't want to create separate pages for each variation. This kind of duplication has the potential to hurt the effectiveness of your overall SEO strategy.

When you have more than one page optimized for similar keywords, these pages may cannibalize each other. Google gets confused—it doesn't know which page to index. As a result, both pages may never make it to the first page of Google, especially for competitive keywords. Google can get similarly confused if internal links between pages have conflicting or irrelevant anchor text. For example, you might have a link on a blog post with the anchor text "Glacier National Park RV park" that links to your "Glacier National Park RV & Camping Resort" page and, while this may have been unintentional, it can hurt your rankings for both pages. Countless times, I've seen an untrained blogger writing and publishing multiple blog posts, all of which are optimized for the same keyword. When asked why they did this, they typically respond, "I thought if I had a lot of pages all optimized for that keyword, we would have more chances of ranking higher on Google for that term." I can't stress enough how damaging that may be to your overall SEO strategy.

Question #4: How can PageSpeed be improved?

The speed at which your website loads, known as PageSpeed, is one of the most underrated technical issues you can address, and it all ties back to one of Google's main goals: provide a good user experience.

As former Google senior vice president Amit Singhal said, "When we slow our own users down, we see less engagement. Users love fast sites. A faster web is a good thing all around."

PageSpeed is critical to the success of your SEO campaign. According to 2018 research by Google, 53 percent of mobile users leave a site that takes longer than three seconds to load. This statistic tells you everything you need to know about why Google takes speed so seriously. It is highly unlikely that your site will rank on the first page of Google for a competitive keyword if it takes forever to load. Nothing kills a user's experience faster than a slow load time. Your goal should be to have your web pages load in two seconds or less.

Fortunately, Google developed a free diagnostic tool called PageSpeed Insights that provides you with a performance score ranging from 0 to 100 for both the mobile and desktop versions of your web page. Please note that the mobile and desktop PageSpeeds are two different scores and should be analyzed and treated separately.

To identify steps you can take to improve your PageSpeed on both mobile and desktop, simply open the tool, enter your URL, and hit analyze. You'll instantly get recommendations from Google on how to reduce your page-load time with proactive measures like compressing images, minifying (removing unnecessary code from) CSS, JavaScript, and HTML, improving server response time, eliminating unnecessary scripts, and setting up a content delivery network (CDN).

Question #5: Is the website mobile-friendly?

More people than ever before browse the internet on their phones or tablets, so if you ignore your website's mobile functionality, you're likely to give a large part of your audience a poor user experience. Because of mobile's popularity, Google rewards mobile-friendly sites and may punish ones that aren't. In fact, in a Google Search Console blog post published on March 5, 2020, Google announced that they would be switching to mobile-first indexing for all websites. What this means is that most crawling will be done with Google's mobile smart-phone user-agent, prioritizing the mobile experience over the desktop experience when indexing content in the search engine results pages.

Any skilled technical SEO analyst should ensure that your website loads properly on mobile: large enough, readable text; accessible buttons and links; correct formatting and layout; and fast load times. To make the issue easy to resolve, Google offers its own free Mobile-Friendly Test, which can be found by searching "mobile-friendly test" on Google.

Question #6: Are there any structured data errors?

"Structured data" refers to a standardized format coded in the in-page markup that classifies page content. For example, it's what tells Google that a recipe is a recipe. Recipe pages tend to all include the same elements: ingredients, cooking steps, time, temperature, nutritional information, etc. When Google recognizes via the structured data that a page contains a recipe, the page becomes eligible to appear as a graphical search result, which means it has a greater chance of showing up on the first page of Google with an image, reviews, ratings, and other microdata.

Google's algorithm understands a page by looking at this structured data, so when errors are present, your page loses the boost of appearing as a graphical search result. In short, structured data errors rob you of quick SEO wins. To analyze and fix these issues, Google offers its own free Rich Results Test, which you can find by searching "rich results test" on Google.

In addition, everything you need to know about schema and structured markup for a service or product can be found at **schema.org/Product** (please note you need to use a capital "P" in "Product" for this URL to work). I'd recommend that you have your SEO team or agency add this to your source code. Then, run the Rich Results Test to ensure that you are leveraging all of the applicable structured data options and confirm that everything was implemented correctly.

Question #7: Is there any duplicate content?

You know by now that Google hates duplicate content. This is why you never want to copy and paste content. For example, you might need a page optimized for "Malibu financial adviser" and another page optimized for "Santa Clarita financial adviser," but they cannot be identical. Swapping out the city name is not enough to get around Google's grudge against duplicate content—the pages must be distinct.

Two scenarios exist where you're likely to see duplicate content without knowing it. First, you might hire a content writer who, in an effort to save time, makes a template and simply fills in a few details for each different page. They might think this is a clever shortcut without realizing the damage it can create to your overall SEO strategy. Second, another website might plagiarize the content on your website and publish it as their own. In this scenario, assuming the guilty website is a financial advisory company comparable to your own, Google should recognize that the content appeared on your website first by the date it was published and cached, and then filter their content out of their index.

But what if an intern at a major news network, a website more trusted and authoritative than your own, intentionally or unintentionally publishes your original content? Google isn't perfect, and in this situation, it might rely too much on the authority and popularity of that website, ranking their page higher than your page in the SERPs.

No matter who steals your content, you can file what's called a Digital Millennium Copyright Act (DMCA) takedown. There's no reason to allow another website to steal your traffic and take credit for something you created.

On the other side of this scenario, your content writer, feeling extra lazy, might decide to plagiarize content from another company's website. As the owner of the company, you may not even know that this is happening, but if you're monitoring your analytics, a significant decrease in rankings and traffic will sound the alarm very quickly. Google takes plagiarism seriously, and if caught using these tactics, your website will most likely be filtered from their index or given a manual penalty. For all of these reasons, it's critical to have someone monitoring your website and your content for internal and external duplicate content problems using tools such as Copyscape and Siteliner. You'll want to address any duplicate content issues as quickly as they surface. There is even a service that monitors your site for plagiarism and proactively files DMCA takedowns on your behalf for a monthly fee. This service can be found at **dmca.com**.

WHAT DON'T YOU KNOW?

With technical SEO, like every other subject, your knowledge falls into three categories: the things you know, the things you don't know, and the things you don't know you don't know.

This third category poses the greatest challenge because it includes subjects and potential problems that you aren't even aware exist. Many technical SEO issues likely fall into this category, and if problems like these go unnoticed, no matter how much money you are investing in your SEO each month, you probably will not see positive results or a return on your investment.

That's why it's so important to have someone proficient in technical SEO auditing, analyzing, and addressing these issues for you. You can't fix problems you don't know exist, but you will sleep better at night knowing that someone who is knowledgeable in this specific skill set is proactively monitoring and addressing technical issues for you.

ARMED WITH THE TECHNICAL SEO BASICS

The issues discussed above only scratch the surface of technical SEO, but you don't need to be a technical SEO ninja. Armed with the basics, you can make better hiring decisions, understand the reports given to you, and hold the agency you've hired accountable so you can see meaningful increases in your site's rankings and traffic. My goal with this chapter is to educate and empower you with enough information to take more calculated risks when engaging or hiring a digital marketing team or agency, and never be taken advantage of again.

As someone who has worked in this field for a long time, I've listened to many stories where business owners were spending thousands of dollars per month on SEO but weren't seeing any results. They didn't know what their agency was doing, nor did they understand why it wasn't working. In fact, most had hired and fired multiple agencies over the years who promised them the world but failed to deliver results. Listening to these stories makes me cringe because it gives all SEO practitioners a bad reputation. This was my inspiration for writing this book. Hopefully, that cycle of disappointment can end with the knowledge you have now.

→ "Technical SEO" refers to the functionality of your website: URL structure, crawl errors, PageSpeed, mobile readiness, and more.

→ You don't need to become a technical SEO expert yourself, but you should know enough to hold the specialist you hire accountable.

→ Google Search Console is your most valuable tool in terms of technical SEO because it identifies technical problems with your website and allows you to communicate with Google.

→ Your technical SEO team or agency should be proactively monitoring and analyzing, and fixing your website whenever technical issues surface.

→ By resolving any technical SEO issues you encounter, you can fine-tune your SEO strategy while gaining a competitive advantage in your market and increasing your rankings, traffic, and sales.

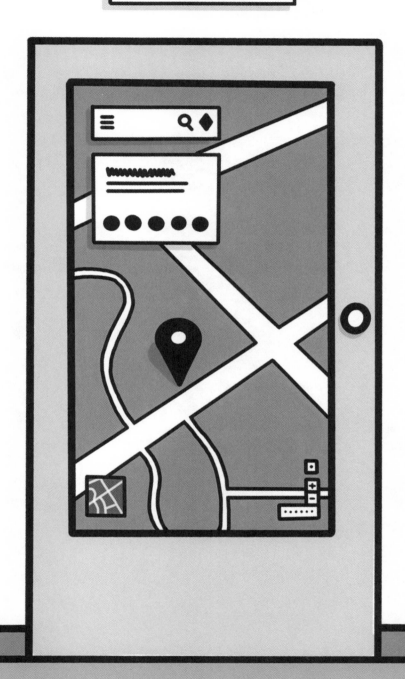

CHAPTER 11

Getting onto Google Maps

When you're looking for a new pizza restaurant or hair salon, how do you find one? If you're like most people, you probably pull up Google and type those keywords into the search box. In under a second, Google's algorithm uses location data and the three components of relevancy, popularity, and integrity to scan its index and create a customized list of search results. Then, the first thing you see on that results page, above every other link, is Google Maps.

Potential customers use this same process to find your product or services. They often reach out to stores or businesses in their immediate area first, which means if your business isn't listed on Google Maps, you could be missing out.

If you're a local business with a brick-and-mortar location or you work from home and serve within a selective radius, this chapter is for you. If you operate an e-commerce shop, or you don't have people coming to your office and you're not geographically tied to specific places, then skip this chapter.

CLAIM YOUR BUSINESS

Your first step to get onto Google Maps will be to claim your company's business listing. Chances are that Google has already created a bare-bones page just waiting for you to come and fill it with more details. Start by going to **google.com/business** and creating a Google Business Profile account.

Google Business Profile is Google's local listing–management platform where you can edit your profile, list your business address and hours, manage and respond to customer reviews, add photos, and get access to your local analytics, among other things. Create an account and start managing your profile as soon as possible because, right now, Google is relying on its data aggregators to pre-populate your business listing.

You need to prove you're actually the owner to claim your business. This is to prevent a competitor or someone malicious from taking over your page and creating problems for you. For example, if someone listed a fake address or responded aggressively to reviews, it could considerably damage your professional reputation.

Google offers two ways to claim your business. The first method is opting for Google to call your business at its publicly listed phone number, at which point they'll call you with a confirmation code to verify your listing. You'll then need to enter the code into your Google Business Profile account. For the second method, which could take up to two weeks, Google will send a physical postcard to your business's location. Similar to the first method, the postcard will have a confirmation code that you need to enter into your account to verify your listing. Google may or may not give you a choice in which way you claim your business.

FILLING IN YOUR LISTING DETAILS

Once you've verified and gained access to your business's account, you can start to fill in the details and complete your profile. Your Google Business Profile listing includes the following:

- Description
- Photos
- Videos
- Address
- Website link
- Business category
- Contact information
- Questions and answers
- Customer reviews
- Hours
- Social media profiles

Fill out as much as possible and leverage every small tool Google gives you because its algorithm values and rewards businesses that have completed profiles and are actively making updates. It wants to see you engaged with the process, so the more details you add, the better.

It's equally important to update your listing if any of your company's details change, like location or contact information. I've seen too many companies lose potential business because they spent years with a defunct phone number in their local listing. Whenever something changes, go into your Google Business Profile account and update the data manually. The algorithm, unfortunately, isn't sophisticated enough to reliably pull information from your site and keep your listing current, so updating should be part of your regular SEO maintenance.

NAP must match

The first details you should check and adjust, if necessary, are your company's name, address, and phone number, collectively known as NAP. If you take one piece of advice from this chapter, let it be this: **make sure the NAP on your Google Business Profile listing matches the NAP on your website**.

Wherever you have your company's name, address, and phone number listed on your website, whether it's your contact page, footer, or anywhere else, it *must* be identical to the NAP on your Google Business Profile listing.

Your NAP details should be identical to what your corporation name or business license displays, and it should match with the chamber of commerce, the Better Business Bureau, and other places it appears. Everywhere your company is mentioned, your NAP should be consistent. If your company is called Joe Smith Accounting Firm, *that's* how it should be written everywhere, not "Joe Smith Accounting Firm" some places and "Joe Smith, CPA" other places.

Google's algorithm grows more intelligent by the day, but you still don't want to risk confusing it—or potential customers, for that matter—with inconsistent details. The more inconsistencies your listing has, the lower your chance of ranking high on Google Maps. The best practice is to maintain consistency wherever your NAP gets published.

Add local schema to your website

After ensuring NAP consistency, your next step will be to add something called "local schema markup" to your website. Local schema markup is a type of structured data code (discussed in the previous chapter) added to your website that identifies local data when Google crawls your site. It's a way to communicate to the algorithm: "Here is verified information that belongs on our Google Maps page. This is our address, this is our phone number, etc." You can think of schema as a little tag that site visitors can't see, but Google's crawlers pick up on it in the source code and derive valuable information.

Hire a Google trusted photographer

Similar to Google Street View, which provides interactive panoramas from positions along many streets in the world, Google also has a program that will bring a trusted photographer inside your business to capture a 360-degree panoramic virtual tour. Not only do the photographs look great and provide prospective clients a preview of your office or store, but the virtual tour also gets connected to your Google Business Profile profile. This is one of the most trusted citations you can get in terms of the Google local algorithm. To find a Google trusted photographer in your area, simply go to **google.com/streetview/busi-ness/trusted/** and search for someone near your office location.

Engage with your reviews

Reviews are one of the most important local ranking factors that contribute to whether or not you will show up in the maps for a localized keyword. Google has also gone to great lengths to weed out fake or paid reviews, and it values when businesses respond to customers.

For this reason, whenever your business receives a review, whether positive or negative, you should always try to respond to that review within 48 hours. If it's a positive review, thank the customer for their business and for sharing their experience. If it's a negative review, don't get argumentative or go into detail about the problem. Remember, these reviews and your responses are publicly visible. Instead, simply say that you're sorry they had this experience with you, and you'd love to rectify the situation privately.

Google monitors and analyzes the reviews businesses receive and the words and phrases people use play into the algorithm. It all contributes to the larger goal of defining the context and relevancy of your business. For example, if a client writes, "I enjoyed working with Chiropractor Frank Smith. He helped me feel better after my motor-cycle accident," Google learns from it. It sees keywords such as "injury," "back," "pain," and "relief," and adds each of these algorithmically to bet-ter understand the relevancy of your business and your local profile.

The more reviews on your listing, the more keywords it will con-tain, so always encourage past customers to add their perspectives. Try to get a review from every single client. You can even semi-auto-mate the process of soliciting reviews by using a service like Podium, which will contact clients after your business interaction through email or SMS. Often, all you need to do to get a review from someone is simply to ask.

Remember, reviews directly affect your local search ranking, so it's always helpful to be proactive and engage with clients. The content, keywords, and review rating all factor into where your law firm may appear in the Google Maps results.

Pay attention to insights

After you've filled out the details of your Google Business Profile list-ing, you can immediately begin to glean useful feedback from the platform's insights dashboard. This page will show you a wide array of details about how users interact with your listing:

- What search queries lead people to your listing?
- Where are visitors located? Which zip codes?
- How many people have viewed your photos?
- How many people have clicked the link to get directions to your office?

When you review these insights, you can learn about users' behavior and adjust your listing and other content to better serve them. You might find that certain zip codes attract more potential customers than you realized, or your listing's activity increased when you added more photos. The point is the more data you have, the better.

MANAGING DIFFERENT OFFICE LOCATIONS

I've already discussed creating individual pillar pages for the different markets you serve, but there are a few more SEO actions you'll want to take if you own multiple office locations.

For each location, you'll want to create the following:

- Google Business Profile listing
- LinkedIn page
- Better Business Bureau listing
- Chamber of commerce listing
- Tracking phone number

I recommend using distinct tracking phone numbers for different office locations, which allows you to attribute incoming phone calls to their respective listing. Even if you have a single office or call center responding to every call, you can tell where the customer is located based on which number they use.

Fortunately, you can maintain different tracking numbers without creating the NAP problems I describe above. Google Business Profile gives you the option to list these tracking numbers for each location while still keeping your official business number consistent.

GOOGLE BUSINESS PROFILE INFLUENCES
YOUR OVERALL SEARCH RANKING

Let me ask you this: Which type of business would Google list first? A business that has ignored its profile and only has outdated data pulled from other sources, or a business that has full contact details, features photos of their office, and engages with customers?

Knowing how your Google Business Profile listing works, I'm sure you can see how the second business goes much further in advancing Google's goal—to provide a good user experience. That's why your Google Business Profile listing affects your website's overall search ranking.

The algorithm looks at everything: client reviews, photos (which I discuss in greater detail in the next chapter), how consistent your NAP profile is across the web, how many people have clicked "get directions to your office" from your Google Business Profile profile, and other user behavior signals that Google monitors. Even without the SEO impact, having your contact and business details readily available is a powerful way to direct potential customers to your business.

If, after optimizing your Google Business Profile profile using all of the tactics we discuss in this chapter, Google continues to populate the local results with companies that are closer to a given location, don't be discouraged. Sometimes, proximity will win out over the quality of the listing. Google will only recommend your company to a certain radius of users, but by putting in the time and effort to make your listing robust and engaging, you can expand that distance as far as possible.

CAN I USE A VIRTUAL OFFICE FOR A GOOGLE BUSINESS PROFILE LISTING?

The short answer to this question is yes. However, proceed with caution. I can count on 100 hands how many times I have heard a business who was using a virtual office complain that they were either not able to show up high on Google Maps or that their Google Business Profile listing got suspended. Some of these businesses were legitimately working out of a virtual office, while others had set up dozens of virtual offices in an attempt to game the system.

Per the Google Business Profile guidelines, "Listings on Google Business Profile can only be created for businesses that either have a physical location that customers can visit or that travel to visit customers where they are. If your business rents a temporary, 'virtual' office at a different address from your primary business, don't create a page for that location. Businesses can't list a 'virtual' office unless that office is staffed during business hours by your business staff."

While this may seem nebulous, I can say with great certainty that a shared receptionist who is not on your payroll does not qualify as "your business staff." Don't get me wrong—I have seen businesses fly under the radar for years and get away with having a Regus or Davinci virtual office as their Google Business Profile profile. While there is nothing illegal about it, just know that in the likely event it does get suspended by Google, the damage may be irrevocable. You could lose all of the time, money, and resources you put into optimizing that location, and you may never see those positive reviews ever again.

Here are some other tips based on my professional experience:

- Do not use a P.O. Box as an address for your Google Business Profile (GMB) profile.

- Avoid using a shared, co-working, or virtual office for all the reasons mentioned above.

- Never let another company that has the same type of business rent or lease a desk or room from you. If they set up a GMB listing using the same address and the same category as you in their profile, that is a recipe for disaster.

- Keep your name, address, and phone number (NAP) consistent on your website, your Google Business Profile listing, and all online business profiles, citations, and directories.

- If you work from a home office, you can set up a service-area Business Profile using your home address, but be sure to hide it in the settings. However, it is exceedingly difficult to rank in the local maps for competitive keywords and phrases using this method.

WHAT IF MY GOOGLE BUSINESS PROFILE LISTING GETS SUSPENDED?

If your Google Business Profile listing does get suspended, don't panic. Sometimes making a slight adjustment to your profile will trigger a suspension, even if you are following Google's guidelines. My suggestion would be to find someone who has experience filing reinstatements because these can be confusing and complex. Remember, time is money, and the longer your listing remains suspended, the longer your business and bank account suffer. At Hennessey Digital, we have reinstated hundreds of these Google Business Profile listings over the years, and each case requires a unique strategy and incredibly detailed documentation.

In preparation for a Google suspension, which will most likely happen at some point, I suggest having the following documentation readily available. This will save you time and increase the speed at which your business listing gets reinstated.

- Set up a LinkedIn page for each office location.
- Have a Better Business Bureau (BBB) membership and profile for each office location.
- Take photos of permanent, branded signage that may include your business name on the outside of the building, on a street monument sign, within the tenant directory in the lobby, and on the inside entrance to your office or suite.
- Have photos of other images as proof of your business's name and address that may include letterhead, business cards, business license, city tax license, or documentation from your secretary of state for each office location.
- Have wide-angle photos of the interior of each of your office or store locations.
- Hire a Google Trusted Photographer to capture a 360-degree panoramic virtual tour for each office or store location.
- Take a lot of photos from your smartphone with your GPS location settings enabled and then post them to your Google Business Profile account for each office or store location. These coordinates are stored in the image file's EXIF (exchangeable image file format) data and share location signals to Google.
- Create a seamless video of you standing outside of your building. Pan the camera across any signage on the outside of the building with your name or the building number, and walk into the building while showing your business name on the

building tenant directory in the lobby and going up any stairs or in an elevator to your suite. Pan the camera on your signage on the outside of your door. Move through your office where your receptionist greets you while recording any other proof that you are located at this address (i.e., your business cards or letterhead with your address on it).

- Make sure that the address on the state incorporation document matches the address of your main headquarters.
- Need more help? You can pose questions and even get answers from community experts at **https://support.google.com/ business/**.

TIPS AND TAKEAWAYS: GOOGLE MAPS

→ Your first step to get onto Google Maps should be claiming your business's listing. It likely already exists with basic information.

→ Fill in as many details in your listing as possible: description, photos, videos, address, website link, business category, contact information, questions and answers, hours, and social media profiles.

→ Make sure your company's name, address, and phone number (NAP) are consistent on your website, Google Business Profile listing, and across the web wherever your business is listed.

→ Respond to both positive and negative reviews within 48 hours after customers leave them. Always be professional and helpful.

→ View insights from your Google Business Profile dashboard so you can learn more about potential customers' behavior and proactively increase your rankings and sales.

→ Create separate pages for different geographic office locations.

→ Avoid using virtual offices, if possible.

→ Always be prepared for a Google Business Profile suspension with photos, supporting documentation, and even a video.

CHAPTER 12

The Importance of Photos and Videos in Your Strategy

Google's artificial intelligence can perform incredible feats, and one of the most impressive is the ability to analyze an image and recognize what it shows. The software, called Google Cloud Vision, can "look" at a picture and tell if it contains a person, guitar, dog, or any other recognizable subject. It can even read the emotions on a person's face and speculate whether the subject feels happy, sad, angry, or surprised.

Why does this matter for your SEO efforts?

If you understand how Google interprets your visual media, you can leverage photos and video to create a stronger association between your website and your chosen keywords.

HOW DOES GOOGLE SEE?

Google analyzes photos using artificial intelligence (AI), but we aren't talking *The Terminator* here. The program doesn't have glowing red eyes. According to Google, Cloud Vision uses "powerful pretrained machine learning models" to understand and interpret images. It assigns labels to pictures based on millions of categories it has learned before. Not only can the AI detect objects and faces, but it can also read printed and handwritten text, identify popular places and logos, and predict whether content needs moderation.

Google's AI constantly grows better and more adept at identifying images. Every time you search for something on Google, you're helping it learn. For example, if you search for "guitar lessons," a list of search results will appear, and you'll probably click on one of the local business listings. There's a good chance the company's logo might contain a guitar or their reviews include photos of people holding guitars. When you click on the business, you tell Google that the pictures are relevant to "guitar lessons," and its understanding of what a guitar looks like grows a little stronger. It connects the keyword "guitar" with the images.

Once the AI has learned to recognize a guitar, the association goes both ways, and it can find photos of guitars all across the web and attach the "guitar" keyword to those websites.

LEVERAGING IMAGES ON YOUR WEBSITE

Google's association between images and keywords means that you can choose which keywords get attached to your site by thoughtfully choosing the photos that appear on your web pages. These images can live on web pages, in a photo gallery on your website, on your social media pages, or on your Google Business Profile listing.

For instance, if you are a personal trainer and post a photo of your business card, diploma, or the front door of your office where your logo appears, Google's AI will read the text in the image: "personal trainer," "fitness," "health," and so on. Every visual word or subject the AI can identify will get associated with your website. It's worth it to include relevant photos on your web pages instead of leaving them text-only because of the visual SEO benefit.

Choosing the right images

You can now see the benefit of using images on your website, but how do you decide which photos to use?

Collect some photos you're thinking about using and try Cloud Vision for yourself at **cloud.google.com/vision**. Using this tool, you can upload the image you're considering and see exactly which key-words Google associates with it.

Let's say you're an auto repair company and have two photos of damaged cars. You run both of them through Google Cloud Vision, which shows you the keywords Google recognizes. For the first photo, the AI returns "car accident," "crash," "car," "bumper," and "repair." The second photo returns similar keywords, but not "car accident," "crash," "repair," or any other terms directly related to repairing vehicles. Using this information, you might choose to use the first photo because it will strengthen the page's association with "car repair" more than the second photo.

The idea is to strategically select images that will best optimize your web pages to rank higher on Google for your target keywords.

Gain keywords through image labels

business_office.jpg

Google's AI recognizes subjects in images, but you can help it along and add additional keywords to your site by strategically naming the files. For example, instead of calling your image files "image_1," "image_2," "image_3," and so on, optimize them with keywords, like "Phoenix car accident repair," "auto body repair," or "auto repair." These optimization techniques provide additional context for Google to understand your content.

In addition to file names, you'll also want to add thoughtfully worded *alt text*, which is the text read by screen readers and other accessibility devices that describes an image for people with sight limitations. It's also a good idea to add captions, the text that appears below or alongside an image to provide greater context.

Source high-quality photos

My next suggestion is to invest in high-quality images instead of relying on stock photos, especially if you're uploading them to Google Business Profile or other pages where they might be misconstrued as your own.

Google knows if an image is a stock photo originating from Shutterstock, Adobe, or any other stock source on the web. For this reason, I recommend taking your own photos, either by hiring a photographer (like the Google Trusted Photographers I describe in the previous chapter) or simply using your smartphone. Take smartphone photos around your office and you'll get the added benefit of having geo-coordinates attached to the images that prove they came from your company's listed location. Remember, Google values authenticity as a way to separate spammers from legitimate businesses. Taking your own photos tells Google, "We're a real business. Our address is what we say it is. This is what our office looks like." Sending Google this reassurance that your business is legitimate will increase your rankings, traffic, leads, and sales.

Creating a better user experience

Gaining keywords from Google is half the reason you should make photos a part of your SEO strategy, but the other equally important half is that images create a better user experience. People respond to visual information, and images break up chunks of text in a visually appealing way. This makes the text easier to navigate, and images—whether they're photos, graphs, charts, or diagrams—can supplement text to provide additional context and information.

However, one trend that can lessen the user experience is for company owners to put their face all over their website. Using your face isn't always a bad idea—people respond emotionally to faces and seeing a photo of the owner can build feelings of trust. But make sure you're satisfying the intent of the user first when deciding which images to include on a page. If a potential client searches for "real estate agent," think about what they want to see. What conveys the message, "We're here to help you find the home of your dreams"? The overuse of the agent's faces can instead say, "This is all about us, not you," which is not the message you want to send.

As I've emphasized throughout the book, Google prioritizes great user experiences. If you can use visual imagery to enhance your design and provide a better user experience, the algorithm will reward you for it.

Images can drive traffic to your website

Another benefit of website images is they can drive traffic to your website. Imagine that you've hired a professional photographer to take photos of exotic floral bouquets at your florist shop. Once those photos get uploaded to your website, they'll also appear in Google image search if optimized correctly. If a user searches for "flower arrangements," they might see your photo and click on it, which would take them directly to your website. Another indirect benefit is that images are shareable in a way text isn't, and people may link to the pages that contain them, which will lift your Google rankings.

LEVERAGING VIDEOS ON YOUR WEBSITE

Videos, while similar in their benefits to photos, have a few unique strengths worth discussing:

- Videos can convey complex ideas and topics to visitors.
- Videos capture visitors' attention and keep them on the page longer.
- Videos are more entertaining and appealing than reading for many visitors.

Video's ability to keep site visitors on your page longer is especially beneficial for SEO. Google's algorithm doesn't listen to or watch videos; it merely relies on signals to determine relevancy. Remember, Google gauges relevancy in part by measuring how long users view content after making a search query before going back to Google and clicking on a different search result. Moving too fast back to Google is called "pogo-sticking." If a user stays on a page instead of pogo-sticking off of it, Google reasonably concludes that the content satisfied the user's intent for that particular search. It strengthens the connection between the web page and any keywords contained in the search term.

Don't embed videos using YouTube

It's best practice not to use YouTube's embedded links to add videos to your website. When you use a YouTube-embedded link, a site visitor will often interact with the video and click over to YouTube. Then the visitor is on YouTube watching music videos or the new trailer for *Star Wars*. They didn't spend a lot of time on your page, which sends behavior signals to Google that your content may lack relevancy for that specific search query and negatively affect your search rankings.

The goal with videos is to convey information to users while keeping them on your page until they convert. For this reason, I recommend a video hosting service called Wistia. Wistia lets you embed videos without linking to external sites. That means when someone watches a video on your page, you have their full attention, which increases the chances of converting that visitor into a lead. Wistia also gives you detailed analytics about your videos, so you can see which videos are holding people's interest, where people tend to skip ahead in each video, and more.

That being said, I still strongly encourage you to create a YouTube channel and post your videos there, as well. YouTube is the second-largest search engine in the world; only Google is bigger. Millions of people use it every day, so you definitely don't want to miss out on their viewership.

In fact, I recommend posting your videos to several video hosting websites because each platform is another potential link pointing back at your site. Not only are multiple video hosting sites important to your link-building strategy, but they can also attract different viewers. Some users might frequent YouTube, while others watch videos on Vimeo. By covering all of your bases, you put your videos in front of more potential prospects.

Apply video schema markup

In the chapter on Google Maps, I discuss how local schema could be used to format your content in a way that fits Google's formatting standards. It allows Google to better understand the data contained in your content and increases your chances of ranking in the featured snippets.

Video schema markup works the same way. It's snippets of code you can add to your embedded videos that assist the algorithm in understanding your content. Using schema, you can give Google the following information:

- Video title
- Description
- Thumbnail image
- Video length
- Transcript

Using video schema markup makes Google more likely to feature your video in the carousel of video results at the top of the first search engine results page, and it will increase your video's overall visibility.

Create compelling thumbnails

Many people choose books by their covers, and it's the same with videos. When publishing videos, you want to create or choose compelling thumbnails. When choosing videos to watch, people gravitate toward faces, so this is one area where using people in your images fits the best practice.

INVEST IN YOUR PHOTOS AND VIDEOS

A picture is worth a thousand words, and a video might be worth a million. They should both be a fundamental part of your SEO strategy. Not only do photos and videos add valuable keywords and context to your website, but they also provide a better, more engaging user experience.

Creating high-quality videos and photos is an investment in your site that, while costly, may pay back dividends in increased traffic and converted leads.

TIPS AND TAKEAWAYS: PHOTOS AND VIDEOS

→ Google uses artificial intelligence (AI) to analyze photos and videos for keywords and relevancy, which it then semantically associates with your website.

→ Strategically choose images that will further optimize your web pages for your chosen keywords.

→ Take the extra time to optimize image file names, alt text, and captions with keywords.

→ Invest in high-quality photos that show your real office or store—Google values original, authentic content over generic stock images.

→ Breaking up your web pages with images and videos provides a better user experience and may convey information clearer than text alone.

→ Videos keep visitors on your web pages for longer, which increases Google's relevancy score and your chances of converting that visitor into a lead.

→ Photo and video production can be expensive, but it's worth the investment because it may bring in new backlinks, increase your Google rankings, lift traffic, and generate more leads that turn into paying customers and revenue for your company.

CHAPTER 13

How to Convert Traffic to Profit

Before I share strategies for converting website visitors into customers, I want to remind you that the SEO work on your website never truly ends. It's like the horizon, stretching on forever. You'll need to monitor and analyze your site's performance, produce new content, attract more links, continually optimize, and more. Don't forget that your SEO-savvy competitors are working on the same things, too. There's always work you can do to improve your website.

I don't say this to intimidate you, only to give you a realistic expectation of what it takes to have a high-performing website.

The good news is that after you start investing in SEO, your work compounds itself. The content you write today will continue to generate leads next month and even five years from now. You make a large upfront investment when you build or redo your website and put the SEO fundamentals in place, and it pays off over time. As your website's authority increases, your focus shifts toward growing your reach and maintaining your high search ranking rather than creating it from scratch. Over time, your cost per customer acquisition goes down as your current efforts build on previous ones.

SEO might seem expensive when you're first starting, but I advise you to stick with it. Continue making the investment, and the cost-to-reward ratio will shift further in your favor the longer you keep at it. Your return on investment will continue to grow and compound exponentially over time as long as you continue to implement your SEO strategy correctly.

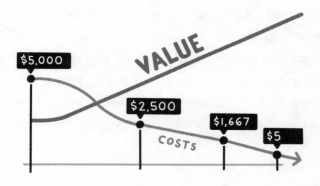

THE LONGER YOU INVEST IN SEO, THE BETTER

To see how your SEO efforts compound, imagine that you have an accounting firm and you've spent $5,000 on SEO. From that initial investment, you generate 500 website visitors. Out of those visitors, two people sign on as clients, meaning you spent $2,500 to acquire each client.

As you publish more content, your website's popularity grows. You spend another $5,000 on SEO the next month, but you attract 1,000 new visitors, of which four become clients. Now that you've spent a total of $10,000 and have six clients, this brings your cost per acquisition from $2,500 down to $1,667.

As you can see, the more targeted content you continue to publish and the more authoritative your website becomes in the eyes of Google, your cost per client acquisition continues to decrease. In a year, your cost per acquisition may only be $500 because the content you published months ago is still generating traffic and bringing in leads. This is where the compounding effect really kicks in for companies that continue to invest in SEO.

CONVERTING WEBSITE TRAFFIC

You can bring visitors to your website, but without a good user experience, they probably won't convert into customers. Your content, messaging, and user experience should convey appropriate empathy, trustworthiness, and competence.

Would you hire yourself?

Let's say you own a window cleaning business. Start by asking yourself, "Based on our website, would I hire us? Does this website make me want to pick up the phone and call?"

Think about what you would want to see from a company if you had someone inside your home cleaning your windows. What questions would you have? What details, qualifications, safety protocols, or calls to action would you want to see?

Ideally, your messaging will include these points and entice visitors to take action. You've worked so hard to implement and invest in your SEO strategy, so now that you have a prospect visiting your website, don't leave such a crucial moment in the customer journey to chance. I recommend personally reviewing your website's content on a quarterly basis. If the content on your website comes across as unwelcoming or confusing for any reason, it might be time to retrain your copywriter.

Make contact effortless

Next, increase your chances of converting visitors by making it as easy as possible to contact your company. Here are a few best practices:

- Display your phone number in the top right corner on every page.
- Code the page so the phone number remains visible, even when you scroll down. The visitor should never have to search for the phone number.
- Put a contact form on every page. It should be short, simple, and require only a single click to submit.

As the saying goes, "A confused mind never buys."

Make it easy for your prospect to connect with you by way of a phone call, simple form submission, or a web chat. By providing multiple options, you increase your chances of converting that prospect into a customer.

Show off your accolades

If you work in the service industry, you never want to come across as bragging, but if you've received awards, display them. Consider how potential customers feel when they are seeking your services—they need to know they can trust you. Awards and recognition make a compelling argument for the service you provide and create confidence for your prospective customer.

Accolades you might want to display include but aren't limited to these:

- Association memberships (YPO, etc.)
- Press (i.e., *Inc.*, *Forbes*, *Entrepreneur*, etc.)
- Professional awards
- High Better Business Bureau rating

Again, visitors look for reasons to trust you—make it easy for them.

Don't leave potential clients hanging

If you're a service-based business, then your business hinges on getting phone calls or emails where a potential client reaches out to you in hopes that you'll solve their problem.

Finally, the moment you've been waiting for arrives: a potential client has picked up the phone and called or emailed you. Now's the time to ask yourself, "Do we have a good system in place to handle calls?"

If phone calls are a primary way of getting business, aim to answer calls within two rings. If a caller gets sent to voicemail, return their call quickly, preferably within the hour. Don't leave them waiting. Respond to form submission leads, emails, and web chats preferably within an hour as well.

I've seen and heard horror stories where a lead comes into a business, and because of internal inefficiencies, the business doesn't follow up until three to five days later. The chances of converting that lead into a client go down dramatically the longer you take to respond.

Let's say you have a leak in your home and you call four plumbers, three of which send you to voicemail, but you speak with one who can be there within an hour. Regardless of whether or not this plumber is more expensive, chances are you're probably going to hire them simply because they answered the phone, were polite, and offered a solution to your problem.

At Hennessey Digital, we recently ran an experiment by contacting 732 of the top law firms in the country via their website forms. Amazingly, 33 percent of these firms took more than one hour to get back to us, and 24 percent of these firms took more than two hours to get back to us. To say these firms are throwing their money away is an understatement. At the same time, 54 percent contacted us in less than 30 minutes. When you decide how important it is to get back to your potential clients immediately, keep this in mind. If 397 of the top law firms can get back to leads that quickly, what's keeping you from doing the same?

In the same way, you'll also want to create an effective intake script your office can use that acknowledges the lead's unique need or situation. You can get as sophisticated as you want with your system and even set up automated text messages to communicate and keep in touch with potential customers.

Using a call center can be a good option as well. I recommend finding one that has experience answering calls for your specific type of business. When evaluating call center companies, ask if they answer after-hour and weekend calls for your company. Additionally, some can prequalify leads, provide immediate information, or even finalize sales for you. If you decide to go with a call center, my main piece of advice is to make sure you understand their process and are continuously proactive with the intake scripts that they follow. The last thing you want is to invest so much in SEO only to lose a potential customer forever because of one bad phone call.

A chat service can be a solid alternative or addition to hiring a call center. Available 24 hours a day, the chat service can answer basic questions and collect a site visitor's information so you can follow up with them during business hours.

For all of these suggestions, apply discretion. If you're a plumber, being immediately available on the phone matters. But if you're a wedding planner, then many of these guidelines might not apply. The most important thing, of course, is that the reason you're doing SEO is to help you get leads and turn them into paying customers or clients. Whatever way they choose to get in touch with you should be handled effectively, leave a good impression, and increase the chance that they'll convert.

Make your website accessible

Another important factor to consider for conversions is accessibility. Not only should your website be usable by everyone so you don't turn away potential clients, but you're also legally bound by the Americans with Disabilities Act (ADA) to provide accessible services. Many large companies have lost lawsuits costing millions of dollars because their websites weren't accessible to people who use screen readers, captions, or other accessibility features to interact with the internet.

To ensure that your site remains accessible, I recommend using a service called UserWay at **userway.org**. It's an accessibility-compliance solution that helps ensure your website meets ADA requirements. The plugin will do things such as enlarge text or read content out loud without you needing to hardcode changes into your website. It's a quick and easy way to make sure all visitors can access your content and services, and it decreases your liability for a potential lawsuit.

LEARN FROM ANALYTICS TO OPTIMIZE CONVERSIONS

At the end of the day, you can speculate about what you *think* is working in terms of your SEO strategy and the return on investment, but why leave that to an educated guess? Let the empirical data help you make more concrete decisions with your strategy to drive more traffic to your website and convert that traffic into more revenue for your firm.

The data is available by looking at your website analytics. Discover what drives conversions, which search queries produce the most leads, where potential clients are calling from, and more so you can adjust your tactics accordingly. You might need to change your processes in one area, redesign a web page in another, or double down on practice areas that net you the most leads or profit.

I mention analytics throughout the book, but here are a few metrics that are particularly useful when studying conversions.

Call tracking software

Most call tracking software solutions have dashboards that allow you to track all the calls that come into your company. You can listen to calls, see how long they lasted, track lead attribution, and even see the zip code where a call originated. Make the most of call tracking by using dynamic number insertion (DNI). This allows you to assign attribution to inbound calls using specific phone numbers that dynamically display on a web page, depending on the source of the visit to that page. For example, your visitors will see a different number depending on whether they came to your website via a Google organic page, pay-per-click campaign, Facebook, or any other traffic source.

Again, keep in mind the nature of your business. If getting leads on the phone is an integral part of your company, then this is important.

If you sell mostly online training courses, then it wouldn't be, and there'd be no reason to do this.

Funnel placement

Funnel placement means figuring out how invested or involved a potential client was before converting them into a client. Where were they in the funnel that goes from the general public to signed clients?

For example, did they visit your website once and immediately call to set up a consultation? That means they were higher in the customer funnel. Or did they visit your website several times, watch your videos, and read your white papers before calling? If so, they were lower in the funnel.

Someone else might visit your website and leave without contacting you. This person abandoned the funnel, and seeing where that happened can indicate that the web page or piece of content where they left needs to be more engaging.

Perform A/B split tests

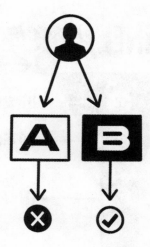

To take a sophisticated approach to comparing different conversion-point options—like two versions of a contact form—try A/B split testing.

A/B split testing involves creating two versions of a web page, one with option A and one with option B, to see which performs better. For example, you might find that over the same period of time, Contact Form A, which says "Request a free consultation," resulted in 100 leads, while Contact Form B, which says "Request a consultation," resulted in only 50 leads. After performing this A/B split test, you now have quantifiable evidence that Contact Form A outperformed Contact Form B and lifted your conversion rate by 100 percent, just by adding the word "free." Even if one option only boosts your conversion rate by 1 percent, that difference can add up to an appreciable amount over time.

There's no end to the different site elements you might compare using an A/B split test, such as:

- Images
- Calls to action
- Button text
- Size and placement of phone number
- Forms
- Design options like fonts and colors
- Content
- Page titles

Running A/B split tests to see which conditions result in the most leads or signups is called conversion rate optimization, also known as CRO. The more you engage in it, the better your site will become at compelling people to contact your company. Never assume that one design option will work better than another, because design is subjective. Always test and validate your choices to get the best results possible. Let the data tell you what changes to make.

CONVERSIONS COMPLETE THE SEO PROCESS

Gaining traffic through SEO is merely a path to the ultimate goal: gaining more customers. The second half of that equation is to turn that traffic into leads by getting users to take action—pick up the phone, fill out a form submission, or engage in a web chat.

The best way to bring your SEO efforts to a profitable conclusion is to earn your site visitors' trust with a great user experience. Whether it's the strength of your product and its ability to solve their problem or it's you as a consultant simply sympathizing with their unique situation and guiding them forward, create a great experience for the people who choose to do business with you. These are real, living people with families and feelings—the better you can help them achieve their desires and fix their problems, the more business you'll get, the more word-of-mouth you'll create, and the happier everyone will be.

Lastly, remember the SEO process never truly ends. For every potential customer you convert, another two haven't visited your website yet, which is why you should continually strive to increase your traffic and reach. Rely on analytics and data to further refine your processes and improve your website. As your investment in SEO grows, so do the rewards. The more traffic you bring in, the more revenue you'll earn.

→ SEO will increase the traffic to your website, but traffic alone won't make people contact you. Make it as easy as possible for potential clients to contact you, whether by email, phone, form, or web chat.

→ Once people call, have a well-trained intake person or team that follows a proven script designed to treat your prospects with empathy and respect while collecting the necessary information to see how your product or service will solve their problem.

→ Earn potential customers' trust by highlighting your accolades on your website.

→ Don't neglect website accessibility—it could deprive prospective customers of fair access to services and create potential legal liabilities.

→ Continually improve your conversion rate by learning from your data and analytics.

→ Run A/B split tests to determine which of the two options performs better.

→ Lastly, remember that SEO is a never-ending process, and the ultimate goal is to make more sales and earn more revenue.

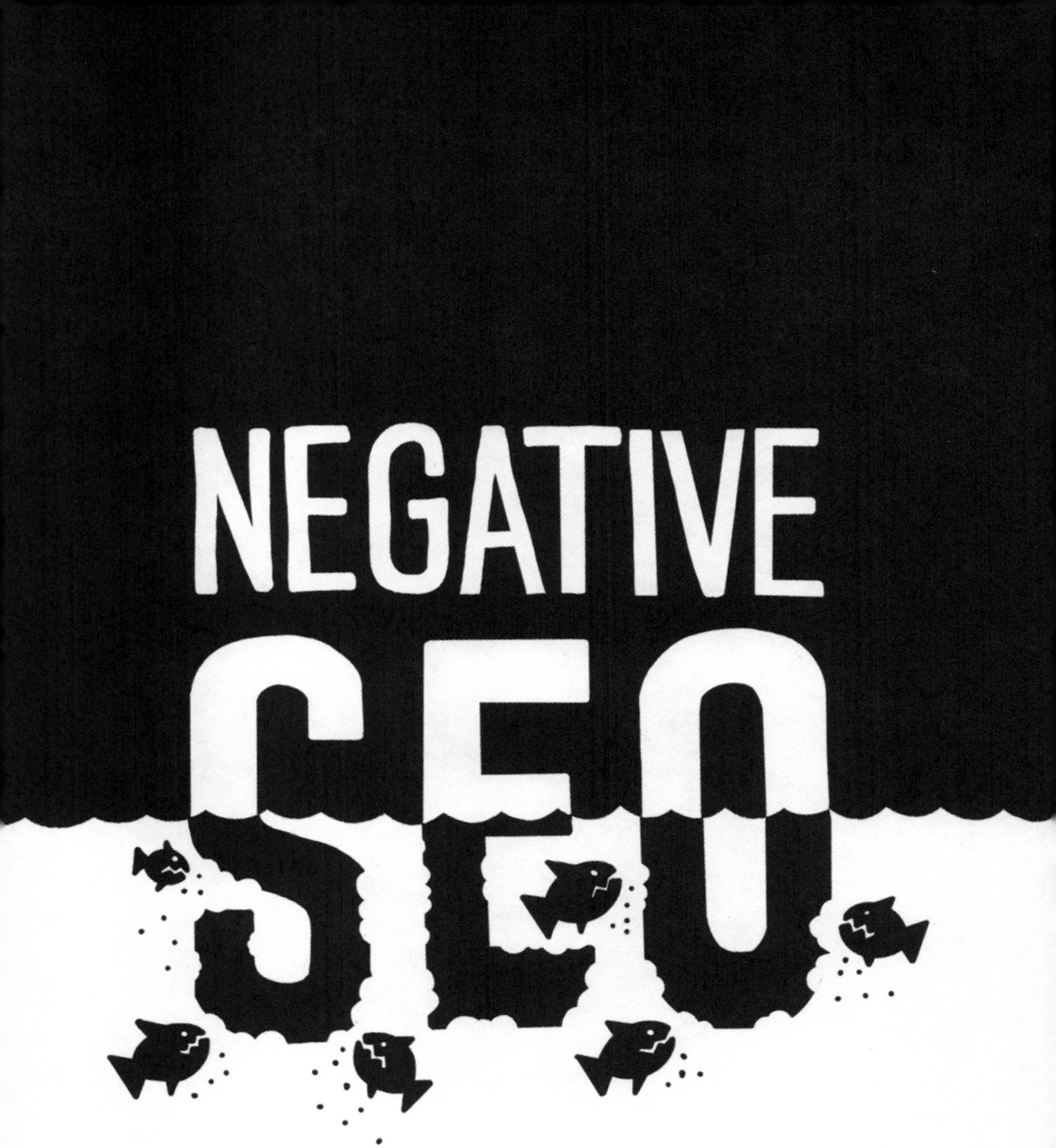
NEGATIVE
SEO

CHAPTER 14

Negative SEO

You've made it—you've fought your way to the first page of Google, and your website traffic has never been higher. Now what?

This whole time, you've been playing offense as you tried to outperform and overtake your competitors' websites. But once you reach the top, it's time to switch to defense. You're the target now, and that means protecting your website from something called "negative SEO."

Negative SEO refers to black hat SEO practices and other malicious actions that people may use to sabotage your Google rankings. If someone malicious successfully pulls off their attack, your domain could even wind up in Google jail. As I discuss in chapter 8, "Google jail" means your website has tripped an algorithmic filter—the result of duplicate content, spammy links, or other unwanted behavior—and received a manual penalty from Google. The consequences of receiving a manual penalty can be devastating, causing a decrease in rankings, organic search visibility, traffic, and revenue. Google gives out these manual penalties as a way to protect users from viruses and vulnerabilities, among many other reasons.

Imagine that your website has been ranking on the first page of Google, but then someone with bad intentions manages to hack it and inject a virus into your code. Now, whenever a user clicks a link on your website, the virus may attempt to extract their passwords and stored credit card information. To prevent users from clicking your links and falling victim to the virus, Google essentially banishes your website to the later pages of search results or may even remove you from the index completely. If nobody visits your site, nobody can get attacked.

However, without the proper monitoring systems in place, you might not even be aware anything has happened. A week or two later, maybe you'll realize you haven't been getting nearly as many leads as usual, but by then, the damage in lost business cannot be recovered.

YOUR NUMBER ONE DEFENSE: GOOGLE SEARCH CONSOLE

Google Search Console has come up multiple times throughout the book, and for a good reason: it's your website's number one defense system. If you haven't already set up the console for your website, then put the book down and go do it right now. It's that important.

Google Search Console is the only way for Google to communicate with you directly and let you know there's a problem. If you get a manual penalty, it will show up in the console. Unfortunately, Google doesn't always provide a great amount of detail, so you might need to do a bit of investigation to identify the issue.

Once you've figured out what's wrong, you'll need to fix the problem and file a reconsideration request. Depending on the nature of your problem, Google might ask you to document the actions you've taken to resolve the issue.

HOW DO NEGATIVE SEO ATTACKS HAPPEN?

Protecting your website means being proactive because an attack can happen in several ways.

Spammy backlinks

The most common negative SEO attack involves building spammy backlinks that point to your website. Usually the attacker will unleash automation software that crawls the internet and builds links wherever it can—links to *your* website. Worse, sometimes the anchor text will contain pornographic or otherwise moderated content that will raise red flags in Google's algorithm and get you in trouble.

Google doesn't know who's building the links, but it may assume that you, the website owner, are engaging in spammy behavior and will then penalize your website. Your search ranking will plummet, and if you aren't monitoring your rankings, links, and traffic, you might not even notice you're under attack.

If your website has a strong, natural link profile with links from trusted sources like *USA Today* and *The New York Times*, an influx of spam links won't instantly destroy your reputation with Google. Google takes your history into consideration, but you'll need to address the problem quickly by using Google's disavow tool to disassociate your website from these toxic links.

The disavow file tells Google, "I didn't create these links, and I want nothing to do with them." Once you've disavowed, Google should block the association. It's like having a party with a security guard at the door checking the guest list and allowing only those who were invited through the door.

Removing good links

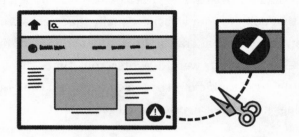

Another attack involves the perpetrator attempting to remove the good links you worked so hard to acquire. For example, they might reach out to the Better Business Bureau pretending to be you and request that the site change or remove the link to your website. Usually they will be unsuccessful, but that won't stop them from trying. The only thing you can do is proactively monitor your new and lost backlinks on a weekly or monthly basis using a tool like Ahrefs.

Outdated plugins

Another common way for negative SEO to happen is via outdated or poorly coded plugins, especially with websites built on WordPress. **I cannot stress how important it is that you keep your plugins up to date if you have a WordPress site.**

Because WordPress is an open-source platform, anyone can access the code, which means there are more opportunities for people to develop hacks and viruses. When this happens, developers push out updates to their plugins to close the vulnerability. If you don't update yours, your website remains open to attack, either by a competitor or an opportunist trying to take advantage of your situation.

If you have a WordPress site, I recommend manually updating your plugins whenever an update gets released. I suggest manual updates instead of automatic because occasionally a plugin update may break your website. For example, your contact form might be a plugin, and if an update breaks the code, you won't get any new contact submissions until you notice and fix the problem. When an update comes out, quickly look at the comments and reviews on the plugin's page, and if everything looks good, go ahead and update.

SEO shortcuts

Negative SEO can also happen to your site because of ignorance and incompetence, more than malice. For example, an inexperienced SEO professional or team might not even realize they shouldn't use automation tools to build links. They think they've found a great tool—until their client's website gets hit with a manual penalty.

Alternatively, they might be under the constraint of a tight budget and feel pressure to produce results. They decide to take shortcuts and use black hat SEO practices with the hopes that they won't get caught. It might even work for a while, but Google is difficult to trick forever.

You can protect yourself from human vulnerability by hiring a reputable SEO team or agency and using the knowledge you've gained from this book to hold them accountable.

Distributed Denial of Service (DDoS) attack

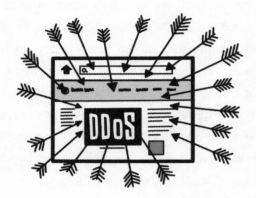

DDoS attacks frequently happen, even to larger websites, and involve flooding the target website's server with traffic. Most websites aren't set up to handle hundreds of thousands or a million visits an hour, so the server shuts down when the traffic hits a certain threshold. While the server is down, visitors can't see or use the website. The longer your website is down, the more traffic and revenue you continue to lose to your competition, and the more suspicious you look in the eyes of Google.

Clone websites

Yet another type of negative SEO attack involves a perpetrator making a clone of your website with all the same content. Suddenly, all of the content on your website registers as duplicate content. With any luck, Google will recognize that your website has existed longer than the imposter and won't punish you. Other times, its algorithm doesn't recognize that the content belongs to you, and it will dock your rankings. In either situation, you'll need to file a Digital Millennium Copyright Act (DMCA) complaint to get the offending website taken down.

To protect your website from plagiarism attacks, I recommend using a service from **dmca.com** that will monitor the web for duplicate content and file a takedown request on your behalf if it finds someone is using your content without your permission.

Fake reviews

You'll also want to monitor for fake reviews criticizing your business. Imagine that you have 10 five-star reviews on your Google Business Profile listing, and then one morning, you wake up to find 40 new reviews with only one star. This influx of bad reviews will crush your average rating. If a fake-review attack happens to you, you'll need to work directly with Google, Yelp, or whichever review site was involved in an attempt to get the fake reviews removed.

Private blog network

Some digital marketing agencies use what's called a "private blog network" (PBN) to build links to your website, but this practice can get your website in hot water with Google if not executed carefully. A PBN is a network of websites, often owned by an individual or an agency. They use the PBN to generate backlinks for their clients and their own web properties in an attempt to increase rankings and traffic.

While I've seen the more sophisticated networks leverage this strategy with great success, those who are less sophisticated can kill the entire SEO strategy and cause their website to get penalized by Google. Google values authenticity. Its algorithm can pick up on patterns associated with PBNs, and when it realizes that you aren't building these links naturally, it may penalize your website.

To protect your company, ask any agency you consider working with whether they use a PBN as part of their link-building strategy. Hopefully, they are honest and tell you no, along with their reasoning. However, if they say yes, then proceed with caution.

Don't get me wrong; I have many affiliate marketer friends who use PBNs, but I wouldn't recommend using this strategy for your company. The risk is not worth the reward in the long term.

Click fraud

One of the most expensive attacks your law firm can suffer is click fraud. In this attack, the perpetrator may use a bot or even people to click on your ads many times using different proxies and IP addresses. This could easily cost you thousands of dollars in wasted budget, depending on the limits you set for your pay-per-click campaign. Google uses live reviewers, automatic filters, machine learning, and deep research to block as much invalid and fraudulent activity as possible, but you should actively monitor your campaign and report anything suspicious to Google.

Gaining access to your site

If someone malicious gains access to your website's code, they can cause a ton of damage. For example, they might de-index your website with Google, meaning your website won't show up in search results at all. Remember, when you see search results, you're looking at a snap-shot of Google's index, not a live, real-time scan of the internet. When this happens, unless you know precisely what to look for in the source code, it can be difficult to identify and fix the problem.

How might someone gain access to your website?

A disgruntled former employee who still has access to your server could go in and break things. Someone could hack your site if you have weak security measures and passwords. Or, if you don't have administrative privileges, an agency or hired professional could hypo-thetically take control and hold your website hostage.

To protect your website from unwanted access, you need protocols in place for handling security. Here are a few best practices:

> **Use secure passwords.** A secure password should con-tain a combination of upper- and lowercase letters, numbers, and symbols. It can be made even more secure by avoiding the inclusion of any recognizable words or names. Whatever you do, make sure that you don't

reuse the same passwords on a bunch of sites. I recommend using a password manager, such as LastPass or 1Password, to make it easy to use unique passwords that are nearly impossible for hackers to guess.

Retain administrator privileges yourself. If you have to burn bridges with an agency or professional for some reason, the last thing you want is for your website to be solely in their hands. You should have administrative privileges to both your website and your server so you can revoke others' access if needed.

Have a system to handle employee access. Along the same lines as the first two practices, you want a system in place for handling security whenever an employee leaves or joins the company. If an employee gets fired, you'll want to revoke their website access immediately. Even if an employee leaves on good terms, don't leave their access open. You have no idea what they might do a few years down the line, and there's no reason to risk your website's security. I recommend using a service like **okta.com**, which provides secure identity management with a single sign-on.

Your website's security is of the highest importance, so make sure the agency you hire has protocols in place to protect it from hackers, vulnerabilities, and malware. Also, make sure that your hosting company has both automated and manual backups to help protect your data, which can be restored in minutes if your website is compromised. Trust me, you will sleep better at night.

ARE NEGATIVE SEO ATTACKS BECOMING MORE COMMON?

You might be wondering how common these attacks are, and how likely it is they'll happen to you. While negative SEO is not a very common practice, as your website grows in terms of authority and popularity, you become a bigger target for these types of attacks. If you're just starting out, your website likely doesn't pose enough of a threat to be much of a target. However, as your PageRank and TrustRank continue to grow and you begin to rank high on Google for competitive keywords, you become more vulnerable to this type of attack.

In most cases, it's not your direct competitors who are engaging in these types of unethical practices. We see negative SEO more from anonymous lead generation companies, spammers, or those working on behalf of a company where the company owner is not aware that these shady tactics are being used. Remember, your SEO success is very transparent to others who may be jealous or vindictive, and they may have no problem using unscrupulous practices to compete.

Unfortunately, there's not much incentive for people to abstain from committing these attacks. By using a tool called a virtual private network (VPN), attackers can obscure their location, which makes it incredibly difficult to determine who is behind an attack. From what I've seen throughout my career, there's approximately a 98 percent chance you'll never catch the person who did it.

Another confounding factor is the tech-savviness of many young people today. Every few months, you hear a news story about yet another teenager who's managed to hack a celebrity's Twitter account or a company's website. Web attacks, in general, are increasing in frequency partly because it's easier than ever to learn how to perpetrate them. With an abundance of free coding resources and a computer in nearly every home in America, the opportunity for mischief is there for anyone willing to take it. People can change the world for the better with computers, but they can also do a lot of evil.

Negative SEO attacks aren't going away anytime soon, so as a company owner, it pays to be prepared and proactive when it comes to your web security and protecting your investment. Establish good practices now, because as the saying goes, "An ounce of prevention is worth a pound of cure."

→ Reaching the first page of Google means switching from offense to defense. Now you must defend your rankings and protect your website from potential attacks.

→ Google Search Console is your best defense against negative SEO. The console helps to provide insights when your website has a problem so you can take quick action to resolve it.

→ Malicious individuals may attack your website in all manner of ways: spammy backlinks, removal of good links, outdated plugin vulnerabilities, black hat SEO techniques, distributed denial of service attacks, cloned websites, fake reviews, private blog networks, and click fraud.

→ Negative SEO attacks will only become more of a problem as young, technologically savvy people grow up with access to free educational resources where they can learn these unethical practices.

→ Proactively monitor your website for attacks and take preventative steps to protect your SEO investment.

Conclusion

You've covered a lot of ground in the last 14 chapters, and you now have a strong idea of the depth of SEO as a field. But I also hope you don't feel overwhelmed. Remember, you don't have to be an SEO expert. By understanding the basics, you're already leagues ahead of most business owners.

You're now armed with the knowledge you need to take action. I recommend going back to chapter 1 and skimming through the book again to create a detailed action plan that you and your team can follow. In fact, I hope you keep this book at your desk and reference it frequently as you carry out and manage those in charge of your SEO strategy. You'll pick up on details you missed the first time and more clearly see how different SEO practices fit together.

ACTION CREATES RESULTS

Only by putting this information to work can you see a meaningful increase in traffic and sales. Much of what I discuss boils down to the two ways you can get more traffic: boosting your popularity with link building and becoming an authoritative source by writing and publishing more targeted content. These two activities deserve the most attention, and they also require the most ongoing work.

However, they will only be effective as long as you continuously monitor, fix, and keep up with technical SEO best practices. As you learn more from experience and analytics, you'll want to monitor your rankings, re-optimize pages, and strengthen content as necessary.

Growth won't happen overnight—SEO is a never-ending process of continual monitoring, maintenance, and improvement. You can't check a box and be done with it. On the contrary, you could have an agency of 100 people working on your website, and they would still find improvements to make. There's always more content to write, more links to build, more conversion factors to optimize, and more analysis to perform. The work never ends, so I encourage you to have patience and celebrate the little wins. Each step forward means more potential revenue.

TAKE ON THE COMPETITION

You're starting at the ground level, and right now, you need to lay the foundation. Today, your website might appear on page 14 of Google, but keep at it—you're playing a competitive game of inches. Before long, your site will be on page 11, then page seven, then four, until one day, you'll see it at the top.

Don't be discouraged by the length of time it takes to develop strong SEO, because you may be competing with companies that have been working on this for years. Give yourself time to catch up. As a business owner, you aren't afraid of competition—you probably thrive on it. Success in SEO is all about studying the competition, reverse engineering their strategy, and then beating them at their own game.

Throughout the process, keep in mind that Google's algorithm is constantly in flux. You'll see setbacks and shifts where your website moves up and down in the search results. This "Google dance," also known as *everflux*, happens to all websites and is nothing to worry about. It certainly doesn't mean you've lost. As long as you consistently provide an excellent user experience, create high-quality content, and manage your website's integrity, your site will be seen as a trusted source of information to Google.

INVEST IN YOUR WEBSITE'S SUCCESS

Whether you build a team in-house or hire an agency is up to you, but in my experience, you'll see better, faster results by working with a full team of experienced professionals. Either way, it's your job to understand what your team is doing and hold them accountable. With the knowledge you possess now, the days of self-proclaimed experts being able to take advantage of you are over. You can and will make your investment in SEO a good one.

The cost of hiring an agency might seem steep up front, but skilled SEO work compounds and pays dividends. It brings to mind a story about a client who went all-in on his investment in SEO. Determined to make his law firm rank number one in his market, we got to work. Our team wrote about 100,000 words of content every month and worked with a large SEO budget. Eight months later, I visited my client in his office because he planned to go out to dinner with the team.

I found him at his desk, face red, with a bottle of blood pressure pills and a stack of paperwork in front of him. "I can't go out with you guys tonight," he said. "I have too much work."

Our SEO efforts had been so successful that the firm had too many signed cases to handle. He was going to have to spend all night in the office filing papers and preparing cases. He looked at me and said, "Is there any way we could just slow down the SEO for a month until I can find more people to hire?"

I had to tell him no, SEO is like a broken fire hydrant, and there's no turning it off. Fortunately, within a week, my client had hired more employees—the surge in cases meant he had the revenue to quickly grow his team—and since then, his law firm has been more successful than ever.

Done well, SEO is the rocket fuel that helps your business launch into the sky. If you follow the advice in this book and execute your strategy right, SEO will help you increase your sales and you'll have to hire more staff to keep up with demand.

I hope you close this book feeling confident and capable of taking on SEO. If you'd like to learn more about working with our digital marketing team, please visit us at **hennessey.com**. *Mention this book, and we'll be more than happy to give you a complimentary website audit to get you started on your SEO journey.*

Acknowledgments

The first person I want to acknowledge is my mother, JoAnn, who had me at 18 years old and sacrificed everything to raise a young child on her own.

Grandma Josie and Grandpa Frank, who both taught me to be kind, humble, and respectful.

To my stepfather, Pete, and my two younger brothers, Peter and Vincent, for always supporting me through all of my entrepreneurial journeys, both good and bad.

Of course, and most importantly of all, I want to thank my wife, Bridget, for your unconditional love and support, even though my crazy ideas almost made us go bankrupt more than once.

To my children, JJ, Zach, and Brooklynn: know that everything I do is for you three.

Cameron Herold, my executive coach and one of the primary reasons I wrote this book. Thank you for passing along all of your wisdom, for making tons of introductions, for holding me accountable, and for helping me grow both personally and professionally. I am truly honored to call you my coach.

Scott Shrum, my "second in command" and one of the smartest people I know—a Jeopardy champ and an MIT graduate with a Kellogg MBA. Had we been in high school together, my grades would have been much better because I would have strategically sat next to you in class. Thank you for your leadership, thank you for proofing this book and for all your suggested edits, and thanks for being a role model to the entire Hennessey Digital team.

Michele Patrick, my CFO. What a dream it is to have you on our executive team. If it weren't for you taking so much off of my plate, with both finance, HR, and stress, as a true perfectionist, I would never have had the time to write this book. Your work ethic is admirable, and I am grateful to be on this journey together.

Kathryn Lundberg, my amazing executive assistant. Thanks for not quitting when I told you that your first project was going to be reading this manuscript, line by line, and basically writing and rewriting each chapter. Thanks for making me look smarter than I really am with your editorial guidance and for making my life much easier by having you in my corner.

Mike Rohde, the best sketchnote illustrator in the world, whose illustrations have been featured in one of my personal favorite *New York Times* best-selling books, *Rework*, by Jason Fried and David Heinemeier Hansson. Thanks for taking on my project and helping me communicate my ideas visually for this book.

Hennessey Digital clients: without you, none of this would be possible. I know you all have so many options when it comes to your digital marketing, and I thank you for entrusting my talented team and me to design, implement, and execute your strategy and grow your businesses exponentially, year after year.

The entire Hennessey Digital team: to quote Steve Jobs, "It doesn't make sense to hire smart people and tell them what to do; hire smart people so they can tell us what to do." I am blessed to have such an incredibly talented team with an amazing culture, who take complete ownership of their specific roles and functions, who teach me new things every day while servicing our clients with white-glove treatment.

The entire SEO industry, for all of your continued collective wisdom, knowledge, and insights. Together, we've created some of the best friendships anyone could ask for. We are a small but fierce industry of people who all stick together.

All of my friends, colleagues, and family: I love you all!

God: thank you for all your blessings, for the strength you give me each day, and for all the people and opportunities that you bring into my life.

Thank you to the hundreds of clients who allowed me to reverse-engineer your digital marketing strategies without even knowing that I was doing it over the past 20 years.

And, finally, thank *you* for investing time in reading this book. While I appreciate you taking the time to read my acknowledgments, I am disappointed that you have not started implementing some of the SEO strategies already. Remember, in life, you have the power to create a future that wasn't going to happen; all you need to do is take action. Action creates results. What are you waiting for?

Index

Bing, 1, 78
black hat SEO, 13–14, 72, 133, 243, 247.
    See also negative SEO attacks
    blogs
    anchor text and relevancy, 130–31
    cannibalizing content, 183
    contributing content to external
        blogs, 94, 137–39
    crafting story and landing on
        relevant blogs, 165
    finding, 94, 165
    graphics designers and, 79
    interviews, 135
    link-building/outreach specialists
        and, 78
    media list, 163, 165–66
    need for strategy, 55
    not neglecting, 110
    pitching stories and building
        relationships, 164, 166–68
    poorly-paid content, 55
    private blog networks, 249–50
    spammy backlinks, 47
BrightLocal, 104
Brin, Sergey, 34
business directories, 2, 77, 136, 140, 205

C

cache: search operator, 92–93
call-to-action windows, 33
call tracking software, 234–35
cannibalizing content, 92, 102, 114–15,
    183
Career Builder, 135
CDNs (content delivery networks), 185
chat services, 82, 97, 229, 231–32, 237
Cision, 166
click fraud, 250
click-through rates, 18–19, 63, 76
clone websites, 248–49
cluster content, 56
CNN, 29, 43
co-citations, 168
community media, 136
competitors, 258–59

analyzing, 59–63, 90–91, 100–101, 136
analyzing backlinks, 136
differentiating yourself from,
    159–60
HTML pages, 62–63
link attacks, 131
out-linking, 139–40
pillar pages, 59
reverse engineering strategies,
    60–63, 100, 111–12, 120, 139, 259
SEO and, 18–19
Skyscraper Technique, 118–19
content delivery networks (CDNs), 185
content spinning, 114
content strategy, 20–21, 109–23
    accountability of digital marketing
        teams, 83
    cannibalizing content, 114–15
    core area of focus, 122
    cumulative effect of content, 116–17
    customers and potential customers
        first, 84
    defined, 4
    fresh content, 20–21, 28–29, 55, 116
    geographic location, 112–15
    goals of, 121
    graphic designers and, 79
    identifying target audience, 111–12
    overcomplicating, 121
    regularity and consistency, 20, 55
    Skyscraper Technique, 118–19
    step-by-step guide to, 120–21
    types of content pages, 110–11
content writers. *See* copywriters
conversion rate optimization (CRO),
    79, 236–37
conversions, 225–39
    accessibility compliance, 233
    accolades, awards, and recognition,
        230
    analytics, 99, 234–37
    asking, "would I hire us?" 228
    effortless contact, 229
    following up on leads, 231–32
    investing in SEO, 226–27
    pop-ups, 33

thumbnails, 221
user experience, 216–17
improv comedy, 162
Inc., 41, 48, 77, 162
Indeed, 135
indexing, 25–26, 28–31. *See also*
crawling and crawlers
defined, 28–29
de-indexing, 250–51
fixing problems, 76
frequency of indexing, 92
mobile functionality, 185
number of indexed pages, 62–63,
90–92
pillar pages, 57
pinging and, 92–93
press releases, 172
publishing new content, 116
technical SEO, 41
variants pointing to canonical
version, 180–81
intake scripts, 232
integrity. *See* technical SEO
internal links, 92, 121. *See also* links
and backlinks
analyzing, 182–83
benefits of, 117
pillar pages, 57
interviews, 135, 140, 168–69
intrusive interstitials, 33

J

JavaScript, 77, 97, 185
job websites, 135

K

keyword density/frequency, 40
keywords. *See also* anchor text
co-occurrences, 168
defined, 18, 61
guest post opportunities, 137–38
identifying target audience, 111
images, 212–14, 216
medium-sized businesses, 71

number of indexed pages with title
tag keyword optimization, 91–92
pages ranking for same keyword,
114, 182–83
pillar pages, 57–58, 120
researching, 70, 100–101, 111, 120
reverse engineering competitor
strategies, 61
reviews, 200–201
Skyscraper Technique, 119

L

LastPass, 252
link-building and outreach specialists,
77–78
LinkedIn, 135, 202, 206
links and backlinks, 79, 127–52, 178. *See
also* anchor text
administrative fees, 137–39
analyzing, 32, 136, 138–39
broken, 31, 41, 77, 102–3
to content that no longer exists, 31
crawl depth, 182
crawl errors, 181–82
defined, 62, 127
disavowing, 98–99, 132–33, 245
goal to build certain amount per
month, 139
guest post link-building
opportunities, 94–95, 137–39
high-quality backlinks, 134–36
internal links, 57, 92, 117, 121, 182–83
link attacks, 131–32
link-building and outreach
specialists, 77–78
link-building strategies, 47, 114,
134–36
monitoring new and lost backlinks,
246
number of, 27, 40
PageRank and, 34, 128, 131
paying administrative fees for,
137–39
pitching stories to gain, 168
popularity and, 41, 59–60, 117

O

Okta, 252
1Password, 252
organic traffic
    defined, 58
    increasing, 63
    measuring, 58
    social media managers and, 78

P

Page, Larry, 34, 93
PageRank (PR), 34–35, 117, 121, 131
    approximating through tools, 34–35
    defined, 34, 93
    growth and vulnerability, 253
    popularity and, 41
    relevancy, 128
    social media, 134
PageSpeed, 76, 184–85
PageSpeed Insights, 96–97, 184
paid media strategists, 78
passwords
    secure, 251–52
    vulnerabilities, 133, 244
pay-per-click (PPC)
    click fraud, 250
    data analysts, 79
    defined, 15–16
    digital marketing managers, 75
    paid media strategists, 78
    SEO vs., 15
PBNs (private blog networks), 249–50
"People Also Ask" feature, 95–96, 120
phones and phone numbers
    business photos, 206, 215
    call tracking software, 234–35
    claiming your business, 197
    displaying number on site, 229
    effortless contact, 229
    media lists, 166, 168
    mobile functionality, 185–86
    NAP profile, 198–99, 202–3, 205
    responding to potential clients,
        231–32
    tracking phone numbers, 202

photos. *See* images and photos
PHP, 77
pillar pages, 56–58, 79, 96, 120
    analyzing competitors, 59
    branching structure, 56–57
    defined, 56–57
    selecting topics for, 57–58
    Wikipedia, 57
pinging
    defined, 93
    promoting caching and indexing,
        92–93
plagiarized content. *See* duplicate and
    plagiarized content problems
plugins
    outdated plugins, 133, 246–47
    pop-ups, 33
    UserWay, 233
    Wordpress, 133, 247
P.O. Boxes, 204
podcasts, 77, 135, 163, 171, 185
Podium, 104, 201
pogo-sticking, 40, 218
popularity, 12, 41–45, 227, 253, 257
    combined with relevancy and
        integrity, 42–45
    Google Maps, 195
    internal links, 117, 121
    links, 41, 47, 59–60, 117, 121, 127–30
    PageRank, 34–35, 41
    plagiarized content, 187
    Wikipedia, 18, 21
pop-ups, 33
PPC. *See* pay-per-click
PR. *See* marketing and public
    relations; PageRank; public
    relations specialists
press releases, 78, 135, 140
    newswire services, 171
    posting press releases on own
        website, 172
private blog networks (PBNs), 249–50
PR Newswire, 171–72
PRWeb, 171–72
public relations. *See* marketing and
    public relations
public relations (PR) specialists, 70, 164

pitching stories, 168
role of, 77
Purple Cow (Godin), 156–57

R

redirects, 41, 77, 102, 180
referring domains, 129–30
relevancy, 12, 25, 39–40, 42–45
  anchor text, 131–32, 140, 183
  combined with popularity and
    integrity, 42–45
  contributing content to external
    blogs, 137–38
  crafting story and landing on
    relevant websites, 165
  defined, 41
  determining, 40
  Google Maps, 195
  images, 212–13
  internal links, 117, 183
  links, 127–28, 132
  PageRank, 34
  pillar pages, 57
  reviews, 201
  thin, low-quality content, 46–47
  videos, 218
remarkability
  believing you are remarkable,
    157–58
  crafting story, 163–65
  defined, 157
  differentiating yourself from
    competitors, 159–60
  doing remarkable things, 161–63
  pitching story and building
    relationships, 168
reverse engineering competitor
    strategies, 60–63, 100, 111–12, 120,
    139–40, 259
  Google algorithm, 5
  identifying target audience, 111
  link-building and outreach
    specialists, 77
  link profiles, 139
  top-ranking websites, 15
reviews and review websites

fake, 249
Google Business Profile, 196,
  200–201, 203–4
high-quality backlinks, 135–36
images, 212
management tools, 104
structured data, 186
Rich Results Test, 187

S

Salamunovic, Adrian, 166
schema, 76, 187
  local schema markup, 199
  video schema markup, 220
scholarships, 135
Screaming Frog SEO Spider
  analyzing competitors, 60
  capabilities and benefits of, 102
  crawl depth, 182
  crawl errors, 181–82
screen readers, 214, 233
scripts
  intake scripts, 232
  unnecessary, 97, 185
Search Engine Journal, 48
search engine optimization (SEO). *See
  also* Google
  achieving goals through, 16, 56
  author's experience with, 2–3, 5–6
  avoiding bad information about,
    3, 9, 14
  avoiding complicated information
    about, 3–4, 9
  benefits of learning about, 9–10
  competitors and, 18–19
  content strategy, 20–21, 109–23
  conversions, 225–39
  costs and pricing for, 17–19
  crawling and crawlers, 28–32
  defined, 1, 10
  digital marketing teams, 17, 55–56,
    67–86
  doing it yourself, 17, 68–69
  features that affect user
    experience, 33
  goal of, 18

Vimeo, 134, 220
virtual offices, 115, 204–5
virtual private networks (VPNs), 253
viruses, 131, 133, 243–44, 247

W

web chat, 97, 229, 231–32, 237
Web Content Accessibility Guidelines
    (WCAG), 105
web developers and designers, 16
    PageSpeed Insights, 97
    role of, 77
    technical SEO specialists vs., 177
white hat SEO, 13–14, 48
"Why Every Entrepreneur Should
    Take an Improv Class"
    (Hennessey), 162
Wikipedia, 18, 21, 57, 122

Wine Library TV, 160
Wistia, 219
Wix, 77
WordPress, 69, 77, 133, 246–47
www., 180–81

Y

Yelp, 104, 136, 249
YouTube, 1, 134, 160
    embedding videos, 219–20
    pay-per-click campaigns, 78
    video editors, 79

Z

ZipRecruiter, 135

About the Author

JASON HENNESSEY is an entrepreneur, internationally recognized SEO expert, author, podcast host, speaker, and business executive. Since 2001, Jason has been reverse engineering the Google algorithm as a self-taught student and practitioner of SEO and search marketing.

His expertise led him to build and sell several businesses, starting with a dot-com in the wedding industry. He founded and sold his first digital agency after introducing his SEO knowledge to a group of lawyers in 2009. In doing so, Jason cemented his reputation as a thought leader and authority on SEO for the legal industry. He also runs SEO industry news site **iloveseo.com**.

A keynote speaker, agency growth coach, and frequent podcast guest, Jason is a columnist for the *Washington Post* and a regular contributor to *Forbes, Entrepreneur, Inc., Fast Company, Newsweek, and Rolling Stone.* He's a recipient of the Gold TITAN Business Award for Entrepreneur in Branding, Advertising & Marketing and has been named a National Law Review Go-To Thought Leader.

As the host of *The Jason Hennessey Podcast,* Jason inspires listeners to get curious together through conversations with business leaders, creators, and entrepreneurs. He records his podcast at Hennessey Studios, a state-of-the-art audio and video production playground for creators located in the Television Academy building in the heart of Hollywood.

As founder and CEO of Hennessey Digital, an eight-figure agency with over one hundred employees, Jason has led consistent growth and been included in the Inc. 5000 list of fastest-growing private companies for the fourth consecutive year.

Jason is a United States Air Force veteran and a New York native. He launched his SEO career in Las Vegas, where he earned a bachelor of arts degree in marketing from the University of Nevada, Las Vegas in 2005. Jason grew his reputation in the legal industry in Atlanta and now lives in the Los Angeles area with his wife, Bridget, and their three children.